An Eerie Silence

An Oral History of
Newark Firefighters at the WTC

Additional books by author:

Firehouse Fraternity Oral History Series:
Volume I: Becoming a Firefighter
Volume II: Life Between Alarms
Volume III: Equipment
Volume IV: Responding
Volume V: Riots to Renaissance
Volume VI: Changing the NFD

The Newark Riots: A View from the Firehouse

Hervey's Boys: New Jersey's First Chinese Community
1870-1886 (And What Happened After That)

Fiction:
The Firebox Stalker
The Hand Life Dealt you
A-zou: A Woman Living in Interesting Times

Children's Fiction:
A Hundred Battles (YA)
A Broken Glass (YA)
Balancing Act (Middle Grade)

An Eerie Silence

Neal Stoffers

Springfield and Hunterdon Publishing
Copyright 2019
www.newarkfireoralhistory.com

First Printing: 2019

ISBN 978-1-970034-27-1

Springfield and Hunterdon Publishing
East Brunswick, NJ 08816

Dedicated to all those who selflessly responded to the World Trade Center those September days in 2001.

Contents

Foreword i

Deploying 1

Operating at Ground Zero 63

Remembering 141

List of Interviewees...................................... 176

Foreword

It was never my intention to separate the subject of the World Trade Center from my general oral history. The experiences shared in this book were originally meant to be a chapter in a book recounting responses of the NFD over many years. However, the scale of events on 9/11, the size of the fire ground, and the complexity of the situation demanded a book to cover the subject adequately. Even though these events occurred in New York City, the enormity of what happened made it a regional emergency. The region around New York City is called the New York/Newark metro area by the Federal Government. Those of us who grew up in north Jersey saw the Port Authority of New York and New Jersey Twin Towers rise in the early 70's and witnessed their collapse in 2001. The towers were part of the everyday northeast Jersey landscape when looking east. The World Trade Center train of the Port Authority Trans Hudson (PATH) line runs for about nine miles from Newark's Penn Station to the station beneath the twin towers. The ride takes twenty-two minutes. The Hudson River separates Jersey City from New York City. Newark sits in the Big Apple's backyard.

Tuesday September 11, 2001 began as an ordinary day in Newark's firehouses. Members of the third tour had begun relieving the first tour an hour or so before the official change of shifts at the eight o'clock time blow. The kitchens would have been filled with guys exchanging information and banter over cups of coffee. The television news was inevitably providing background noise to the morning. Some men from the first tour had left early to get to their part time jobs. Others stayed to enjoy the camaraderie of the firehouse a little longer. By eight thirty the third tour was in sole possession of the house and plans for the day were being discussed, a normal day, the last such day. A new normal was about to begin. At eight forty-five the world changed and the fire service felt that change more than any other segment of society.

At 8:45 American Airlines flight eleven, destined for Los Angles from Boston, flew into the north tower of the World Trade Center. The news was no longer background noise. Every firefighter who saw the images appearing on television screens nationwide instantaneously knew the magnitude of the problems facing the FDNY. Both of the towers stood 110 stories high. Each floor covered an acre. 50,000 people worked in these structures. Most would be at their desks when the plane hit. The FDNY was the largest fire department in the country and its members had trained on fighting fires in such buildings, but that training did not include tons of burning jet fuel.

Newark firefighters on duty watched the morning's events unfold. Most saw it on television. Some went to vantage points around the city to see. They knew the dangers their brother firefighters faced. When a second plane hit the south tower, their frustration grew exponentially. But it was a New York City operation.

Newark could only watch. The collapse of these two behemoths changed everything. All knew that hundreds of firefighters were inside those structures when they failed. The buildings had come down in what is known as a pancake collapse, the deadliest type of collapse. The catastrophe unfolding had instantly surged beyond the capabilities of any single fire department. It was now truly a regional disaster. The immediate impulse of NFD personnel was to begin gathering and prepare to deploy into New York City.

Although dwarfed by the FDNY, the Newark Fire Department is the second largest department in the region. When Mayor Guliani stated that "We need help", Newark firefighters responded by the hundreds. As the emergency response plans of the region were implemented, Newark fire units were dispatched to New York City to cover areas stripped of fire protection by the response to Ground Zero. After the collapse of the Twin Towers, the nation did all it could to assist the FDNY. But on those first days, the FDNY had to cope with the disaster with very limited help. Members of the NFD did all they could to provide that help.

An eerie silence is a phrase used by more than one Newark firefighter who crossed the Hudson River those first few days. Some use it to describe what they experienced while making their way to lower Manhattan. Others use the term when talking about Ground Zero. Eerie is a word that appears in many accounts of what happened on 9/11. The world first responders operated in after the collapse of the Twin Towers was surreal. The memories of those days immediately following that disaster will haunt many for the rest of their lives. Firefighters as a rule tend to internalize their ghosts, keeping them locked away in mental compartments deep in their minds. It is a necessary skill for a profession that sees the power of fire and its effect on the human body. We may discuss it among ourselves with a gallows humor, but behind the morose chuckles there is sorrow and pain. This pain is especially pronounced when a fellow firefighter dies in the line of duty. On September 11, 2001 343 brother firefighters made the ultimate sacrifice fulfilling the oath they took to protect lives and property. Hundreds of Newark firefighters joined FDNY personnel and firefighters from around the metro area and indeed from around the world in a desperate rescue effort to save lives the first few days after the Towers came down. None knew the conditions to which they were responding. They only knew the need.

Deploying

LaPenta: I was here in the firehouse. We worked the night before. We got off in the morning and the officers' union office was upstairs on Mulberry Street with the old credit union at the time. I think Gerard Rosamilia was upstairs and Patty Doherty and Johnny Sandella. They were all coming into the firehouse for coffee, you know, that morning thing. We were downstairs and we were just doing the regular firehouse morning talk. You know, busy night? Yeah, a job here, a couple of car accidents. They flashed it up on the news that a small plane hit the World Trade Center. We look at the TV and me and Gerard looked at each other. That's no small plane. It's the size of the building. The hole's the size of the building. It's not like a Cessna. Well, it just started to unfold then. We were watching it, watching it. Third tour guys were watching it and then the third tour guys go, banged out to a job. Some of my guys were still there. Couple of guys got in the car, started heading home. It's eight o'clock in the morning. And then me and Gerard and I think Johnny Sandella were sitting in the kitchen and we watched the second plane hit. We were like, "Oh my God. This is crazy." I got on the phone and I called those guys on the cell. "Hey man, we got a problem. Come back to the firehouse." So, guys came back. And then we got called to set up at University Hospital. They set up University for receiving victims. I guess they were spreading them out. And they were evacuating Manhattan via the ferry. So they were originally going to send us over to University Hospital to do that. I believe the third tour wound up going and setting up a decon tent and stuff like that. We were watching the TV, myself and Jay Noble and Stevie Dagna and Tommy Melillo were there. We were watching it and I said, "You know how many thousands of people are going to be dead here?" I mean this is just insane. So I don't know who decided. We were calling people to say, "Hey, we got to go over there. We got to go." This is just crazy. It's like sitting on your front porch watching your neighbor's house burn to the ground and you're not doing anything. Then the first tower came down and I just turned around. I said, "There's going to be a lot of dead firemen. We're going. Let's go. Whether they bring us the truck or not we're going." So we literally piled in the back of my pick-up truck. We took equipment. We took masks. We just took shit from the firehouse. We're like, I'm not waiting for the chief to say go ahead. We're going. And my friend at the time, George, worked for the Star Ledger. He was calling me, calling me, calling me. "Where are you?" I said, "I'm in the firehouse." He says, "I'm around the corner." "We're going over." He says, "Can I come?" I said, "Yeah." He jumps in the front seat and that's how we got those photographs. He was with us the whole time.

The thing that sticks in my mind was walking down Church Street. You could hear a pin drop in New York City. And the dust and the dirt, it looked like a Norman Rockwell winter night painting. It was a bright blue sky, sunny day. When you got into lower Manhattan it was like a snow storm. The dust particles and the debris just floating in the air, the blue sky was completely blocked out. You're walking in ankle deep of dust. It looked like snow, you know. It looked like that dirty snow. And it was silent.

Langenbach: I was in the Arson Squad at the time of the Trade Center and I was working nights. Nights for the Arson Squad were seven at night until three in the morning, sometimes four. Depended on what was going on. So I was working nights. At the same time my mother-in-law was going back and forth to University Hospital for cancer treatment. I would drive her in because I was working nights and bring her back home again. Well, this day I said, "It's time you guys learn how to get there on your own without me, just in case." So, they're driving, my sister-in-law and my mother-in-law in one car and I'm following them in my city car. We're going in up seventy-eight into the city and I hear a radio report of a plane hit the Trade Center.

It's early in the morning, of course the first thing I thought of was, Piper Cub flew out of somewhere, crashed into the building. It's bad, but it's not that bad. So we're going along and then I hear a second plane hits. We're almost in the city now, a second plane. At first I thought it was double reporting on the same incident, but then it turned out to be two different towers. So now I know I'm going to work. I'm not going to be going anywhere. I'm going to go straight into work.

I'm just waving to them and they're waving back. And I'm going like this, "No, no, I have to go to work." And they're going, "Hi." So finally I went by them at about a hundred and fifty miles an hour, just kept on going into the city. I get into Newark and first I go to the squad and check in there and then I go to the Emergency Operating Center, which is on Washington Street. And I check in there. Now I'm in a really wild shirt with I think I had jeans on or something. I'm into the ops center. Everybody of course is looking at you. Now they're all in uniform. You can imagine the hub bub that's going on in there. I sit there and try to get a sense of what's going on. I don't know how long I was there, probably like an hour or so. I walk down to Lee's was right there by Washington. I walk down there and buy a white shirt and get him to put on a patch for me and I come back. Now I still have my jeans on, but at least I have a uniform shirt. I feel a little better.

Because I wasn't going to go back home. So I was sitting there, again trying to get an assessment of what's going on. You could see all things, people gearing up, the hospitals are gearing up. Everybody's gearing up for this whole whatever this is going to turn out to be. A report comes in, this is early on. A report comes in; a report of a suspicious van in front of the Rodino Building with drums in the back and wires. So this is, you could imagine, the wheels are really turning now. So I bolt out of there with somebody else from the Newark Police SWAT team. We go down there and there's this poor Ecuadorian man spread eagle over the hood of the van with a Federal Protective Services cop with his MP5 pointed at him. What's going on here? Thank God I talk enough Spanish to get by. He was from Ecuador. He was a seaman on a ship from Ecuador, an Ecuadorian flagged ship that was in Port Newark. They set him into town to buy some lubricating oil. He's got the lubrication oil in the van. There wasn't anything to the wires, but he got lost and he stopped of all places in front of the Rodino building on this day to ask directions. So they cut him loose.

Get back to the EOC and now things are starting to ramp up all over the place. A call comes in from NYPD to NPD and the Prosecutor's Office looking for post blast people. People who have been trained in post blast investigation to come over to the Trade Center. So we put together a quick squad. It was myself, Ray Irizzary, Nate Johnson, and Nelson Perez from our guys and then a detective from the Prosecutor's office and we went over.

We went down Two-Eighty to the Holland Tunnel and were escorted through. We were met there by Port Authority Police and were escorted through there. Everything was shut down. It was kind of eerie. We went right down the Westside highway. Met there with some people then we went back up to Javits and met some people at Javits. Then we go to a public school close to the Trade Center. We met there and that's where we met with the squad from NYPD. We went to work with them right away.

There's a whole group of people and it's all bosses, Deputy Chiefs, Battalion Chiefs on the fire side, Inspectors from the Police side and a lot of civilian people around. It's like an Emergency Operating Center. And they're all going back and forth. Well, this poor fire chief, he doesn't know how many people he's lost yet. But he's lost a lot of people. He's up there and he's trying to get things organized because I guess they deferred to him to be the Incident Commander. He's having a hard time getting people to listen. This grizzly Police Inspector gets up and says, "Okay, number one, everybody shut the fuck up. Shut the fuck up." And he puts his arm around the chief and he says, "Go ahead boss, what do you want to say." So then the chief does what he wants to do and he goes, "I got to know how many from the Medical Examiner's side. So this guy gets up and he's a civilian now. He's all puffed up. He's going, Well the New York City Medical Examiner's Office is prepared to do blah-blah. The grizzled Police detective goes, "Hey, I don't give a fuck what you're going to talk about. Just tell me what you can do. What you got right now. How you're going to get it to me. How we can use it." And that's the way it went for the rest of the meeting. We got introduced to him a little later on and he says, "Alright, I've got work for you guys. And he sent us to work with the NYPD squad.

Bellina: Yeah, I was actually working the night before. I got off. And I went home, pulled in the driveway, and my son Frankie was a senior in high school at the time. He was crying. I said. "What's the matter? What's going on?" "You know, dad, there's something going on. It's on the news. A plane hit the World Trade Center." I wasn't listening to the radio or anything on the way home. So, I said, "All right calm down. Just go to school. Everything's fine, you know, it's an accident. What are you going to do?" I went in, he came inside with me and the second plane hit. My wife was actually the manager of the cafeteria at Bishop Ahr High School. I said, "Tell your mother I'm going back to work. I'm not staying here. There's something going on here. This is impossible." I wind up at Twelve Engine.

That's where I was at the time. I go into Twelve Engine. Everybody's watching the news. And the two buildings are still up and we're talking about it. My God, what's going on? And then the buildings collapse. So we're watching it on the news when they go down. So we're like, "Oh my God, there have to be hundreds of firefighters that are trapped in this stuff. What are we going to do? We need to do something." So, being the person that I am, I called dispatch and I said to a chief dispatcher, "Can you do me a favor. Can you call all the firehouses and find out who wants to go to the World Trade Center." He goes, "What are you an idiot? I'm not doing that. You're not going anywhere." And hangs up on me. Well, I hang up the phone over at Twelve Engine so hard that the hotline came off the wall, broke off the wall. I was pissed off. So it turns out that in the process, he calls the director and tells him that this idiot just called and said that he's trying to rally the troops to go over there. The director calls Five Truck because Twelve Engine's line is not working. I just ripped it off the wall. And he goes, "No one's going anywhere. No one's leaving. If you go over there you're getting fired." And I basically said, "Fuck him. I don't give a fuck." My Marine is coming out now. They attacked the United States. I'm not fucking staying here. There're firemen over there. I don't know what I'm going to be able to do, but I'm going. So with that we find some people that are going over there. I think there were like twelve of us that wound up going together. Kevin Killeen was one of them. I don't know how we all got together. We get a bunch of equipment, like hooks and stuff like that together and we had our turnout gear. We're trying to figure out where we're going to go and how we're going to get there. We go outside and a PAL police bus was actually outside there. It's in front of the firehouse. Nobody's in it except the driver and there's a police radio in there. I go out to the cop and say, "Where are you headed?

He goes, "I just dropped the kids off. Why? What's up?" I said, "We need a ride to Liberty State Park. We want to go to Liberty State Park." I don't know this, but somebody's saying, "Frank we could probably get across at Liberty State Park with a boat or something." So I tell the guy. He knew what was going on. He was listening to the radio. "Hold on. Let me check with my boss." So he calls on the radio and his boss says, "Absolutely, take them." We get on the bus. We highjack this bus. We have no permission. We got a city vehicle that's taking us to Liberty State Park. I remember traveling down Seventy-eight. There was no one on the road, no one. And I remember seeing the smoke in the distance. One of the guys said, "I'm nervous about this. I'm not good with dead bodies." So I said, "Don't worry about it. It's going to be okay." We're having a discussion as we're getting closer and closer. The bus pulls up at Liberty State Park and they got these columns in front of us. You can't drive any further. And in the distance I see firemen in a different color turnout thing, they're wearing a tan color. There's probably like fifty of them when I climbed up there. So Chief Killeen goes down and he plays by the rules. Frank is not like that. I'm going to break every frigging rule known to man. So the chief goes, "Let me go down to talk to them." It turns out they're Jersey City firemen. They're being staged. We never were staged for anything. Okay? They're being staged and they're waiting for the command post over in New York to call them in. This has all been pre-planned. They must have done drills So, I'm like, staged? What are we talking about? We're going over there. The chief goes, "Well they told me they're waiting to be called. So I go, come on. I go down there and the Jersey City chief goes, "You got to wait here. This is a command post and we're being staged." Now in the Newark Fire Department at the time, we knew nothing about this structure and what they're talking about. We don't drill. We don't get along with other fire departments. It's just the way we are, right? We're like give me the hose and we'll put the fire out, right? So that's my mentality and the Marine in me is coming out and the aggressiveness. So, I go, stage? Waiting for who to call you? He goes, "New York City." I said, "They're all gone. There's no command post. There's no one over there. The building's collapsed. You're going to be waiting here all day. So, we're going over to help." This guy goes, "You just can't do that." I go up to the trooper on the boat. I go, "Listen, we're from the Newark Fire Department. We're the best in the state." With Chief Killeen standing there I said, "We're going over." He goes, "Okay get on the boat. Twelve of us get on the boat. We sit there. This Jersey City chief's yelling. He's not stopping. He's like, you can't do this. The pilot of the boat comes back out and says, "Listen, before I take you over there I just want to let you know. They think there's anthrax over there." I go, "What the hell is anthrax?" He goes, "It's not good. But they think the jet had anthrax." He says, "Do you still want to go?" I says, "We're going." We get on the boat and I was sitting with my back against the pilot house of this boat. It was a small boat, probably around thirty feet. Wasn't gigantic and only two guys could actually get in to the center of the boat to pilot it. As I'm looking my back is towards this wheel house, and I'm looking out. I could see the Statue of Liberty and I said to myself at that time, "My great grandfather came to this country not knowing anything about what's going on." I don't know why this ran through my head, but here I am looking at the Statue of Liberty. He looked at the Statue of Liberty when he came here, not speaking English, with his family. Me with two sons at home, we were just attacked. What does this mean for me? I'm not worried about where we're going. It's just going to be a mess. I'm worried about tomorrow. I'm worried about my sons. They're going to be in the military. They're going in the military. They're coming right out of high school; they're going in the military. I remember thinking that to myself. As we're going across, there was a fighter jet that came down low. And it was as to say we're here. It was like almost saying the military's here. We got your back. Not meaning for us, just meaning situation wise. So knowing the military, that was the signal they were sending. It just gave me a whole new perspective. When we get to Manhattan, a guy comes with one of those golf Gator type carts that the construction guys work with and he had a paper mask on. We all get on this thing and we go down West Street and we make a right. I guess it was on West Street we make a right. There were no people. All we saw was eight to ten inches of dust and papers and a blue sky and nothing going on. And then when we turn the corner, that's where we saw the devastation. We saw one of the rescue companies that was blocking the road, the lights flashing with dust all over it, smashed. There was a big tractor and the firemen were arguing with the guy driving it, get out of the tractor. You're not moving our truck. We're moving our truck. They would not let the construction worker push the truck over, out of the way. They were doing it. That's the kind of chaos that was going on. And now you're talking about two hours into this. The buildings have been down for two hours if not longer.

Killeen: First of all we started gathering at Five Truck for some reason, like the pirate station. And after a few phone calls we had a group of guys that just gathered. You've got to understand all the traffic has been stopped on all the major highways. It was at a standstill. We got a phone call from headquarters that they were sending somebody down to arrest us so we couldn't go over to the World Trade Center. So at that time we looked at each other and then somebody sees a Police Athletic League bus go by. So they flag it down. And they go, we've got a PAL bus out here and they're going to take us to Liberty State Park. I don't know who flagged him down. We all just jumped on the bus with our gear. We took no tools because we didn't want to strip the city. You know you had no idea what's going on, so we didn't want to take anything from the city. So we just had our own turnout gear and we jumped on this bus and headed over to Liberty State Park. And of course there's a lot of chatter going on, you know. Jerry DeLane was there. Jerry DeLane called a friend of his that's a judge. And the judge said, "Don't worry nobody's going to put you on charges or anything, not today." That part of our mind was cleared up. We get to Liberty State Park and other departments in Hudson County were there with apparatus. They're all lined up; and they're staged; and they're ready to go with no ferry to take them across. So I'm trying to figure out what the hell's going on. A couple of guys scatter around and come running back. Frank Bellina says, "Come with me and think real fast." So I'm running to a dock and I go, "What the hell's he talking about?" We get to a dock and there's a police boat there, a New York City police boat. And they say they're making one trip over and they're not coming back. And we go, "Okay." And he says, "Who are you guys?" So I made up something in my mind. I said, "We're the strike team out of Newark." It sounded good, right? We jump on the boat. There're about twelve to fourteen of us. We jump on the boat. And the cops go, "Before we move, we have no idea if there's anything over there that's like a bio hazard or something like that. We have no idea. So if you want to get off the boat, get off the boat now." Nobody got off the boat. So we all kind of pointed towards New York. That was it. We took this boat to New York. We pulled up to a small dock where they would have pleasure craft down at lower Manhattan. And as we leave the boat, we're still just making this up as we go along. They had a box of little filter masks. So we grabbed one on the way out because we had nothing. As soon as we stepped foot off the dock there's this dust. It seemed to be about maybe five to six inches thick. It was concrete dust. We didn't know it. I'm putting this together in my head. And there're still the papers from the buildings floating around. It's just like snow. It's like a snow storm you're walking through. And out of the snow storm comes a maintenance man on a John Deere Gator tractor that they would use going around picking up the daily garbage. It was just like he came there to meet us. He just happened to be there. We just happened to be there. He goes, "Hop on." It's like something out of a crazy movie. We hop on, get as much as we can on; start going up there. We're walking and riding up to the scene. And so that's how we got there.

Richardson: September eleventh, we were coming off of a shift. We were still in the old firehouse on Irvine Turner Boulevard and we were leaving. I was working my part time, so I had gotten up in the morning and had left. I picked up the plumbing van and went to the job that we were doing in East Orange. I got to East Orange and we were running new base board, running new heat in the house. It's a three family. I remember the people were talking about something on TV. You talked to the people, but you didn't interact with their lives. I was there to do a job and they were paying my boss to do a job and we were doing it. He was meeting me there. He was picking up material. So I was there by myself and turned around. I hear them start talking about the World Trade Center. Their son had been in the Marines and he was going to Rutgers. He was discharged, active reserve. And he was going to Rutgers. So I look at the TV. I'm like, "What the - - -?" So I called up the firehouse. I go, "What's going on?" I talked to Frank Bellina. He goes, "We're setting up guys and we're going over there. I'm like alright. So I called my boss and said, "Look I got to go." He goes, "Alright, I know." He was an Irvington fireman. He's retired. And his son is on Newark, Donny Meier. Don Meier was in Irvington and then Donny came on this job a little bit after me. So I went back to the firehouse. It ended up being twelve of us. I guess phone calls were being made to headquarters and they were saying, "No, to hold on, don't anybody go." Okay? And Frank never took don't do something as the final answer. So, I guess it was Sigano that had gone outside and flagged down a PAL Police Athletic bus going by Irvine Turner Boulevard, Five Truck and Twelve Engine. He flagged it down. So Frank got on the bus and said to the cop, "We have to get to Liberty State Park somewhere, so we can get over to New York." So, he said okay. He called up on the radio and they said okay bring them. So we were now, of course, outside the scope of what's supposed to be going on. It was the third tour was working that day and so Jimmy Weiss took our names. We all wrote our names down, the guys that were going over. So, if anything happened at least he knew who was there from that firehouse. Other firehouses were probably doing the same thing. We thought that we were dealing with us. So the twelve of us got on the bus and we just took our turnout gear. Put our uniforms back on, took our turnout gear and we had gone to the local food store right there. We bought up like soup and everything, all this food in cans and stuff like that. We were going to take this with us because we didn't know what we were going to. We were going to New York City, but we were going to take our own food. And so we brought all this food and everything with us. In a duffle bag that Frank had, this green duffle bag. We shoved all the canned food in there. I had it; he had it; people were carrying it; and we went over. The stupid thing was I had a bottle of water and it leaked in my boot. My feet got wet. We ended up getting to Liberty State Park and they are just lined up. I mean, rescue crews just lined up. It's the pecking order now. "We were here first." "We're going to go." We were the last team off. So Frank turns around, looks at that, and goes, "Yeah, well, we're going over. So he walks down with Chief Killeen and there's a boat sitting there. I don't remember if it's a police boat or a ferry or whatever boat, but there's a boat sitting there. And he comes up to the guys on the boat and says, "We're from Newark. We're the best rescue company here. We're going over." And the guy says, "Well, then you're going to be the last going over because they're stopping it. They're not going to let anybody else." So he turns around and he waves us up. Here we are with our bunker gear and everything like that. But we didn't want to take our shoes. So we ended up leaving our shoes on the PAL bus. And the guy says, "We'll bring them back to the firehouse." Now here I am. I got a boot full of water. Not that my feet don't get wet anyway, but you know I'm starting out wet. So we walk past all of these guys. We got our coats and our helmets and our gloves in our hands and we're wearing our bunker pants and we walk past all these other crews that are standing there. And they're all looking at us like, "Where are you going? You're in the back of the line." We walked up. We got on the boat. Before we left the dock, the pilot said, "We don't know what's happening. We don't know what's over there. We don't know what's in the air and what you're going to be exposed to. If you don't want to go, make that decision." And we all turned and looked at each other and said, "No, we got to go." The two towers were down and we were like, "No, we got to go." And so the guy said okay. He casted us off and off we went. We got to some port we pulled into over there. And we walked up and it was surreal because for one thing it was quiet. You always hear something. The only thing that you heard in the area, in the sky and everything were the fighter jets that were circling the area. That was the only thing that you heard, nothing else. There were some sirens in the background, but the streets were empty. And there was a grey powder everywhere. We started walking and this guy on this Gator thing picked us up and he gave us some dust masks. He says, "Alright, I'll bring you to the pile." And I remember Frank has this bag of food. Now he's looking at it, what am I going to do with this? He goes, "Okay we'll put it here." We threw it under a car. Now a days, people are going to come by and see this bag and think it's a bomb. But we took the thing and we threw it under a car, like it's going to be there when we come back. That was the only thing we really didn't think through. Twelve of us on this little Gator. The thing is doing a wheelie and we drive up.

Pierson: First thing in the morning, I'm checking the aerial on the side of the building and we're doing housework. It was back and forth. Kraemer came running out. He said, "A plane just hit the World Trade Center." I said, "Holy shit. How drunk was that guy? How do you hit that building?" Then he came out, "A second one just hit." I think I'm going to go in. I'm going to watch after I put the truck back in. And we actually went to a fire down by Ten Engine. Fourteen Engine took up; they come around the corner and said, "The Pentagon just got hit." Holy shit, what the hell's going on? We got back to the firehouse and that's when we started guys getting together to get going.

I went over with a group of guys that took the Police Athletic bus in front of Five Truck. We went over, about twelve of us. We had the cop drive us all the way down to Liberty State Park. There was a bunch of Jersey City Units there. We had Chief Killeen, Frank Bellina, Robert Holland, Jerry DeLane, Mike Gibbons, and John Wilson. I think John Agoston, a few other guys. But we went right up to the end of the dock. There had to be at least four or five companies that are staging there. It was probably an hour and a half into it, maybe a little bit longer. A State Trooper boat pulled up at the same time we got up to the dock. And a Jersey City battalion chief stopped me. "You can't go there. You can't come here running all over." I said, "We got a Battalion Chief right here." And Chief Killeen, he looked like he had already come from the World Trade Center. Those guys' eyes got big. Then Frank Bellina says to the trooper, "We're from Newark. We're the best in the state. You're taking us." We immediately walked onto the boat and the trooper didn't pay Jersey City too much mind. He said, "Well, we don't know what's going on over there. I mean if anybody wants to get off. We don't know if there was any kind of chemicals used or anything like that." But I just remember that the Jersey City guys were looking like, "What the hell just happened?" Yeah, so we got over there pretty quickly. And when we got over there, there was a guy happened to be driving on a long golf cart for fire department personnel. He took us up about two blocks, up to the main area. Your main area was huge. And to see New York City Chiefs that were disheveled and looking like they didn't know what the hell was going on. There were still guys digging out guys from fire trucks. I said, "Holy smokes." We knew it was big just from watching on TV. That was something I wouldn't forget. I guess you could call that one my most memorable events.

Alexander: We were working that day. We got off that evening I'm going to say about five thirty. They had a bus out front of Ladder Five. We all jumped on the bus and we went to Jersey City. And right at Jersey City they had a boat at one of the docks right there. We jumped on that and that's how we got over there.

Highsmith: I reported to work the morning the World Trade Center Towers came down. We were on tens and fourteens at the time. When the first airplane hit, I felt it was a terrorist attack. Just by studying politics and stuff so much, I felt it was a terrorist attack. I got a little nervous being a new guy. I'm waking everybody up, getting the attention of everybody. New York's going to need help with those towers. It was one tower. I was sitting there watching this on TV and the second plane came in. Then we were ordered to get ourselves together to protect this city. So we went out to get the fuel, that's when we saw the towers come down. We could actually sit on the rig and watch the towers come down. People just started showing up at the firehouse with their gear. They're going to New York. Being that we were working, Chief Carter and a few other chiefs came down. A lot of chiefs showed up at my firehouse. They were organizing the party to go at six o'clock. I remember Arson saying that we're not allowed to go. An Arson guy showed up taking names, but when we pulled out I think there were about two hundred cars going out. We went down to Bayonne. The thing that I remember, we went to Bayonne to get on the Coast Guard ship. There were firefighters everywhere. I don't know if they were volunteers, other cities or whatever, but Frank Bellina yelled out, "Newark coming through." And the place just opened up. We just walked right onto the ship and were taken right over there. Amazing, it was amazing. When we got on the ship everybody pulls out their cell phones. At the time I was a single father with a daughter at home. And I called her, tell her good-bye. Call your mama. I'm probably never coming back. That's how I felt. And other people were making the same phone call. Everybody was on the phone saying goodbye. And we got over there.

Petrone: The first day we went, I don't know if it was our union or the officers' union, they rented a bus. We were working still the ten fourteens, so we went over the day between our nights. We came back that night; worked; and then I went over again the next day. We took Captain James Pierson's pickup truck. I think he drove in. The following day, I went over I think with the fourth tour. I went over one day with the fourth tour. With Billy Weidle, he's a battalion chief now, and a couple of guys that worked with him. He was a fireman at the time. I went over four days. The last day I went over, I went over again with Pierson, but I'm not positive how we got over there. We took my car or his car. But we went over.

If you were a fireman they kind of waved you through. They wouldn't let anybody through the Holland Tunnel. So when you pulled up there the first day we had the bus. We had no problem getting in.

The second day we went, we were in the back of Pierson's pickup truck and I think there were six of us in the back and the three guys in the front with all our turnout gear. They kind of waved us right through. You parked quite a few blocks away and then walked. When you had the turnout gear they didn't bother you too much going in, as far as searching and everything. As firemen they kind of let you in. Go head in. So we didn't really run into any problems.

Straile: Unfortunately the city of Newark at the time didn't want any of the firemen going over there. But the unions said the heck with that and they got together. We got buses. And we all got on buses at Twenty Engine on Prince Street. There were buses, two or three busloads of guys that I remember went over there. And we were there for several days. We'd stay a day, leave and come back. We did that for a little while, but it was the unions getting involved and taking the firemen over there, doing our thing that we had to do to help out. That was a tough one. But it had to be done.

Freese: I went the first day it happened. My buddy John Sigano drove and we ended up getting through. Cops escorted us in there and everything. It was just almost like having blinders on driving and I wasn't even driving. My heart was racing. I'm thinking. I'm watching. I'm seeing the video over and over in my head again. I remember my little girl crying, telling me not to leave. So I had other things in my head as John was driving. We parked a few blocks away.

Dainty: I was off the job. But I was there. I was there that day. I was there because I was working in Middletown and they have an air truck to fill their own bottles. They have the ability to fill multiple bottles. It has its own compressor on board, filters and all of that stuff. The guy who was in charge of the mask repair shop in New York City had a working relationship with the SCBA unit in Middletown. They used to go up there for parts. We would send them parts that they needed right away if we had it. So they had a working relationship. When this thing first happened, they were under the thought that they were in rescue mode and they felt that they were going to need air bottles. They weren't going to be able to handle it on their own. So they were reaching out. And I went to the Trade Center with them.

We just convoyed up there. It was a very, very eerie feeling driving up the Parkway and Turnpike with no other traffic and just going. There was that truck; I think we had a pick-up truck with extra bottles. I had a gig. So, it was a strange, strange feeling. We went up the Parkway to the Turnpike to the tunnel. We went to the Holland Tunnel. So we didn't have far to go once we came out of the tunnel.

We were actually parked in front of the New York court building or the Federal Court building and the command post was like half a block away from us. So I was there that day. I went back later in the week, went with the guys from Middletown, but they never put us on the pile.

Griffith: At this point I was in the union office, vice president of the union. We had a charity golf outing down at Atlantic City that we were going to. And I remember getting ready for it. It was like ten o'clock. I lived down the shore, so it was get down there. Maybe eleven o'clock was tee off time. And I remember getting ready and I had the news on or it ended up they put the news flash up that everybody saw. A plane went into the World Trade Center. I'm looking at the whole thing. It's a shock. So my wife's doing something and she asks, "What happened?" I said, "Somebody flew into the Trade Center." And I'm saying, "Yeah probably a Cessna or something. Some small plane wasn't paying attention." Doesn't look cloudy, looks nice out, I mean how the hell would you do that? And then the cameras are on there. Now the smoke is getting bad and you see it. "Man," I kept saying to my wife, "They got to get water on to that thing because we're going to have like the Philadelphia deal where they had the collapse with steel. They got to get water on it." Man, look at how hot a day it is, like ninety-four. And it was getting worse and worse, you see it intensifying. I'm saying at some point maybe the standpipe fails because of the amount of fire. You got to shut valves off now, to get water on it. Then as you're talking about that you see the other plane come in. And I remember my wife screaming because she had the TV on upstairs and she yells, "What's going on? What's going on?" Then they're talking about the Pentagon. I can remember Giuliani coming on. He said, "We need doctors, nurses, any firemen we can get, any kind of police we can get. We're going to need help." I remember getting on the phone and I called Dave. And I said, "Dave, I'm not going (to the outing)." He kind of got angry with me, but he didn't realize the magnitude. I said, "No I'm going up north. I'm going to Newark. I'm definitely going to cancel that outing." So I went up to Newark and you know the game. We played three phone calls or less. We got to do this mission in three phone calls or less. When I got up there, a lot of guys were saying we want to go. We want to do this. So, I had heard that the tour that was getting off, there were some guys there that had gotten over there already. Guys from like Twelve Engine, Five Truck and so forth, they had gotten over there. So, I got some information that they got over on the ferry. So I picked up the phone and called New York Waterways Ferry, whatever ferry was leaving Jersey City. I said, "Hey listen, I've got a bunch of guys here that's growing. A bunch of firemen, they want to go over. They want to volunteer. How do we do this?" So they said, "We kind of shut that down. We're bringing people out. We're not bringing anybody back over. Get clearance, you need to call the Coast Guard." I said, "Oh." He goes, "Well, I've got a couple of numbers here." He named them down and then he said New York Ops. I said, "That sounds to me like that might be a good one. Give me that one and give me the other number too." But I took this

New York Ops. Called New York Ops. It's amazing that I got through in the first place because of the telephones and everything. I got through to a Petty Officer Hugvey was his last name. I'll never forget it, sounds like that old cell phone. I called him. I said, "I got eighty guys. We want to get over there. We want to help." He said, "Oh, wow, great. Get to Liberty State Park. We've got ferries going out of there. We'll get you out of Liberty State Park in Jersey City. We'll get you out of there. We'll get something hooked up there." I said, "Excellent. That's fantastic."

I remember talking to some other guys. There was a group of guys up on Belmont Avenue. I can't exactly remember the actual guys. I know I remember Nasta, Mike Nasta was there. And guys started to congregate there. There were some guys that were congregating down neck in a place, so we're trying to get them together. The guys down neck had heard Liberty State Park, so they took off to go there. They got into Jersey City. It was a whole other deal. They got there some way and then they wouldn't let them out. I was riding up to Five Truck to start to get together with the guys. I get a phone call back from this petty officer. He says, "No, we're not sending you there. You got to get to Bayonne, the M O P terminal in Bayonne." I said, "Okay. So, we're trying to get buses. Meantime those guys up at Five Truck were trying to get buses. They actually reached out to the Fire Chief who told them no and that we were not to go. And that if we did go, we were on our own. The city wouldn't cover us. They actually sent the Arson Squad down there to get names. They said you absolutely cannot go. We, being us, decided that things were going to be different. We were on our own time. We're doing what we want to do. And then they told us not to take our gear because the gear belonged to the city. But that's not true because we were buying our own. That was their whole thing. You can't do this. You can't do that. You're not getting any vehicle. So the guys up at Five Truck were working on going through a tunnel, but the tunnels had been shut down by then. When I got up there, I was talking to Mike Nasta. I said, "This is what I got so far. We can get there." So he said, "All right here's what we'll do. We go in cars. We all piled into cars and we were actually broken down. There were chiefs there. Norman Esparolini was the highest ranking guy there and all the way down. And so there were captains, it was firemen, and we actually broke into groups. So there would be three firemen, four firemen with a captain. And then we had battalion chiefs that took care of the groups. So we actually had it pretty well organized on paper. Guys started to do that and organize it. So we said, "Well get in the car." We got in the car to get on the Turnpike to exit fourteen to get out to the extension. We got there. The State Police had it shut down. We said, "We're a hundred and ten. We're all Newark firemen. We're going over there. We have clearance. We're supposed to go to the M O P terminal in Bayonne. We're going to pick up a boat there. At the Coast Guard station there and the boat's going to come and get us." He said, "Okay, does everybody have IDs?" He went down and he looked at everybody's ID in the car. The Troopers were there. They escorted us to the exit. We get to the exit, the Bayonne exit. They had two snow plows with cops with long guns. And we said we're going to go. He said, "No, we got it shut down. And the State Police said, "No, these guys are going there." There was a little bit of a bickering back and forth, but they got us down there. The trooper actually escorted us all the way down to the M O P terminal. We get there. There're two sentries at the Coast Guard station holding M-16s. So I come walking up. I remember Don Gilmartin was there. He walked up and they said no. So he said, "Eddie this is your show. They're not letting us in." So I called Petty Officer Hugvey. I said, "They're not letting us in. They said there's no boat. They're not letting us in." He said, "Take this phone over to them and tell them to have somebody come out. They're not going to take the phone from you, the two sentries, but tell them to call. Ask for their petty officer or somebody to take the phone back to the highest ranking guy there." I tell them this is Petty Officer Hugvey. He wants to talk to you guys. They yell for a guy to come out. He took my phone. They went inside. They came out. They said, "We don't know who you guys are, but there's a boat coming for you." Now also there was a van of nurses and doctors that pulled up. They were told to come there as well. And then that group that was down neck that went over to Liberty State Park, a police officer had confiscated a bus, a city bus from Jersey City. Threw the people off, confiscated the bus driver and got them there because we told them where we were going to be. That whole group showed up. They were twelve, so then it pushed the number to about a hundred and twenty-five guys. And a boat came. It was a Merchant Marine boat from King's Point, the Merchant Marine Academy, a military boat. We all got on the boat. I remember John

Centanni was there, Chuck West. I was kind of grouped with them. The guys were all fired up; we're going to New York. We're going over there. Everybody's all charged up. You know how that is. We're going to go in. We're going to help and we're going to do things. We're all on the deck in turnout gear and I'm thinking, "Wow, this is a big boat and all, but I don't think they have life jackets for everybody here." But nobody really seems to be concerned about that. It's just one of those deals we're doing.

I remember pulling out and coming around the Statue of Liberty and you're looking. To me when you look back, the scene would be something out of the movie Escape from New York, when New York became a penal colony, but it looked like the whole place was on fire. The big thing I noticed was the silence and the silence was no planes. There was no air traffic which you take for granted all the time, but it was eerily quiet. As the boat came out, a black hawk helicopter came in, had its guns trained on us, talking over the PA and I guess the VHF radio. Told them, "Stop. Where are you going? What's going on?" And then the pilot of the boat says, "Who's the guy?" They were asking where are we going? I told them we're a hundred and twenty Newark firemen. We have nurses and doctors here. We're coming over. So they said, "Well where's your point of entry?" They were originally saying Battery Park, but I kept hearing it was jammed up there, different guys talking here there and everywhere. And I had remembered that there's a boat that leaves out of a marina there. I said the marina that's outside. The pilot of the boat looked down at his chart and gave him the name of the marina. I said, "We're supposed to go right in there." That makes sense. You're right there. And so that was like right at the foot of Liberty Street almost. There's a marina there. I kind of knew that and we said we're going there and they talked back and forth and they said okay. As the boat kept going, guys are talking, guys are talking. You're getting closer and you're looking at forty and fifty story buildings rocking and rolling. I remember John Centanni saying to me, "We shouldn't do this." Just the magnitude, it's like are we getting in the way here? You have the greatest intentions in the world, but wow, this is even bigger than we imagined. This isn't going and putting out a three story frame. This is serious stuff here. We pulled up and just as we pulled up, Seven came down. We were getting off, we were on the dock and the dust came through. We were gagging and coughing. We hadn't done a thing yet.

Roberson: I actually was in the union hall at that time. I saw it on the news and on my way to work coming down Twenty-two I saw the second plane hit. I was like, "That's like the World Trade Center." So when I got in the office the phones were going crazy because everybody wanted to go over there. So we got notices from the state, listen nobody do anything because we don't even know if there's going to be other attacks. We can't send our guys over there and something happen over here. So, all the dust settles around eleven, twelve o'clock. We had to find how we're going to get there. How we're going to enter New York to help the guys there. We coordinated with the state and Jersey City. And we were able to get a boat to pick up a bunch of guys from Liberty State Park over to the

World Trade Center dock. We got about twenty-five guys to go over initially for that night. Everybody else was on standby. We made phone calls. Called everybody on the fire department, be on standby, be ready to come to Newark if you have to. So we did that. It wasn't until two days later that I went over to volunteer.

The funny part, I had my old military flight suit, so I wore that over. Because when you went over you couldn't wear your turnout gear over there. You have to be careful with your turnout gear because it's contaminated. So I had my old flight suit on. I guess they must have thought I was a general or something. They were like, come on, come this way, come right through. I'm like, no problem.

West: I was there numerous times, but the most important time was the actual September eleventh. Third tour, which was the tour I was working on, was working that day. It was a ten hour shift. We were actually watching it from a vantage point that we could see it while we were working. Then when we got off at six o'clock at night, I'm going to say approximately forty of us from different tours, we all met up at the Clinton Avenue firehouse which was relatively new and somebody had a connection and was able to commandeer a Coast Guard cutter to get us over there. I think we had a few vans, different cars. We met down at the Coast Guard off the water. I'm not sure how they got us onto this boat because I'm certain they weren't really supposed to be doing that. But we all got on there with our gear and took a slow trip over to the New York side. I'll never forget it. It was very eerie. I've never been a military person or in war or anything like that, but pulling up to New York City with no electricity. It was very, very eerie. So it was approximately forty, maybe fifty Newark firemen on this Coast Guard cutter on September eleventh. And we went over there approximately seven, eight o'clock at night.

The other times I went over, early on you weren't allowed to drive through the tunnels. So you had to show your badge. We drove our own cars and piled a bunch of guys into them. We made our way over there. I probably was over there five or six times early on. I believe if I remember correctly, you just flashed your badge and they were allowing you to come through. But otherwise they weren't allowing regular traffic.

So you went there as much as you could and tried to help or do whatever you could to make a difference. But at some point I think they all realized that there wasn't any more saving going on. It was just a recovery process. I think they found that out pretty early. So you went over there and did what you could. Being a firefighter, you did what you could do to help.

Willis: Well, me and my mother-in-law were actually watching from the roof. We saw the first one and my mother-in-law, not knowing anything about the fire department, she said, "Jim don't you find it odd that an airplane on a clear day like this hit a building?" And that struck a chord in my head. I went, "Wow, you're right, Ma." We're talking and all of the sudden the second one hit. I looked at her and I told her, "I got to go." She went, "What's the matter?" I said, "This is not a coincidence, Ma. Something's wrong. I don't know if it's war. I don't know what it is. But something bad's going on." Went down, watch it on the TV. The Pentagon, Shanksville, all of that was coming through at the moment I was getting all my stuff together. Called my family and let them know. I wanted to get the kids out of school and have people starting to get ready in case we have to head to Pennsylvania to get out of here. I was really worried. I went to the Academy. Got all my stuff together and went to the Academy.

I wind up running into firefighter Billy Melodic. Billy's been on since 1971. Me and Billy made our way down to Jersey City. Stepping onto the boat, we were ordered by the chief from the Jersey City fire department to get off the boat. That Mayor Sharpe James had called them, notifying them to remove any Newark firemen trying to go over to the World Trade Center. Well, we were having none of that. There were Jersey City Police officers. They said, come with us. They commandeered a bus. Put all the Newark firemen on the bus. Took all the people off and put us on the bus and drove to the Bayonne terminal. They had a Coast Guard cutter that was driving men back and forth. There were about twenty of us that got on that bus, brought us to Bayonne, and we got on the Coast Guard cutter there. We drove over and he dropped us right at the atrium, we dropped right in Ground Zero. I wind up taking orders from Chief Esparolini. He gave orders out to everybody; wanted everybody to stick together.

Centanni: So, I'm a captain at Twenty-one Engine. We're studying for the battalion chief's test. And we're actually just in the midst of studying Brannagan, a building construction book. Bobby Rommeihs and myself and our crew are watching this on TV. We both look at each other. These buildings can fall down. These buildings can fall down and this is how our morning starts. When the building comes down, it comes to me; they just lost our whole department. And we're talking. We're watching, up on the roof, the building coming down. In any event we're watching it unfold; we want to go. Shortly after that, mid-day, we get a phone call from Deputy Chief Dunn. And at the time, I was involved with the union. He reached out to me because we had people self-deploying. Dunn calls us to tell us, "Listen, nobody can go out there. I can't have people leaving work."

That something came down from the county, through the director, nobody could deploy out there. Actually Mike Gibbons was out there already. Mike left with a couple of guys from Five Truck. He calls us maybe mid-day. Tells me, "You guys got to get out here, man. When you get off your shift, you got to get out here. People are just dead everywhere. Firemen are just gone and trapped."

So there was an organized effort. I think we met on Belmont Avenue at the time. Eddie Griffith was very instrumental. He got us over to the Bayonne Naval Yard. He knew somebody in the Coast Guard, had two boats that were going to be shuttles for bodies. They had a field morgue set up there. They weren't doing anything because there weren't many bodies even removed at the time. So, he has a hook there. We meet there and Norman kind of organizes the effort. He assigns captains and makes platoons and groups. You know the accountability thing. We got a sign in sheet of this group. You're running this group, John. You're running this group. We get over on the boat, two boat loads of guys. We brought masks with us, hooks. You know, we're ready to go. We're going over on the boat and it was the most eerie thing in the world.

Two boats are going over together and we're looking at the city. Half of it's black, dark or fire burning and helicopters zipping over our heads. At that time I didn't even own a cell phone. Richie Gail's in the boat with me. He's in my group and I say, "You got a phone? Rich give me the phone." I called home. I talk to my wife. I call my mother and father. I was like, we're heading over there. I don't know what's going to happen to me. Just wanted to talk to you. I was like, this is scary. I don't know if we're coming back. This is like you're going to war. I called and spoke with them. We get over there. Short ride, it's no long ride across the river, right? So we get over there and we get off. It's a dock for yachts and stuff, right by the World Trade Center.

Gail: I was working a day shift when the World Trade Center was attacked. We were watching it live on the news and we were actually watching it from the roof of the building that we were working in. You could see it. That night we got off at six o'clock. A bunch of us mustered up with our gear and we went over there kind of on our own. We all took our cars and were escorted by the State Police to Bayonne and got on a Coast Guard boat. The boat took us to lower Manhattan. That's how we got there because everything was kind of shut down, tunnels, bridges. You couldn't really get in or out at all. So, we parked in Bayonne and the boat took us over.

West: Third tour, which was the tour I was working on, was working that day. It was a ten hour shift. We were actually watching it from a vantage point that we could see it while we were working. And then when we got off at six o'clock at night. We went over there approximately seven, eight o'clock at night.

I'm going to say approximately forty of us from different tours, we're all at the Clinton Avenue firehouse which was relatively new and somebody had a connection. Someone was able to commandeer a Coast Guard cutter to get us over there.

I think we had a few vans, different cars. We met down at the Coast Guard off the water there. I'm not sure how they got us onto this boat because I'm certain they weren't really supposed to be doing that. But we all got on there with our gear and took a slow trip over to the New York side. I'll never forget it. It was very eerie. Pulling up to New York City with no electricity, it was very, very eerie. So it was approximately forty, maybe fifty Newark firemen on this Coast Guard cutter on September eleventh. I was there numerous times, but the most important time was the actual September eleventh.

Prachar: I was on vacation. The first tour worked September tenth, so my guys were still sitting in the firehouse when the planes hit the twin towers. I was home doing landscaping in the backyard with my wife. It was probably ten o'clock in the morning, ten of ten in the morning. The phone rings and my wife answers it. It's my mom. I get on the phone with my mom. My mom says, "A plane just crashed into the World Trade Center." "What?" "A plane just crashed into the World Trade Center." I come running in the house. I turn on the TV. Well, the second plane had already hit and they're re-playing it, replaying it, re-playing and I'm just watching this. I pick up the phone. I call the firehouse. I call Chief Killeen. I call Five Truck. What's going on? What's going on? Are we going over? Well there's so much going on. They decided they're going over. They hear about Liberty State Park. So, I don't get a phone call. Then I call and Chief Killeen tells me, "We're leaving." I said to my wife, "I got to go." So I pack a bag. I'm getting ready to go. She tells me, "Call your mother." "No, I'm not calling my mother." "Call your mother. God forbid something happens to you and your mother didn't talk to you. Call." So I pick up the phone. I call my mother. My mother starts crying, the whole bit. You know, she's getting weepy. I'm getting weepy. Kids are in school. I don't even have any way to say anything to them, but I got to go. I throw stuff into a bag. I go out the door. I stop at a pizzeria. I order like a hundred dollars' worth of stuff. Shoot to the firehouse. Well, Belmont Avenue, ground zero for the Newark Fire Department. Loaded with guys. What are we doing? How are we getting there? They're not letting anybody through the tunnels. You can't go on the bridges. We talked to the guys that went over earlier. They're not letting anybody on boats. So we're back and forth, back and forth. Who's calling this one? Who's calling that one? We got to get over there. In the meantime, I guess Jimmy Weiss was there. Everybody was there. Nasta's coming on duty that night.

Ray Wallace is up in headquarters. Ray calls the firehouse and he's talking to Jimmy Weiss. They're opening the Emergency Operating Center the next day. They need officers to staff it on overtime. Are you interested? Nah, nah I'm not interested. So Ray says, "Are there any other officers?" "Oh, yeah, Johnny Prachar is sitting right here." He hands me the phone. Now in the meantime there are people all over the place. First thing Ray says, "Ah, John I hear a bunch of guys are trying to go over to the city." I had already gotten the word that headquarters says we're not supposed to go over there. "Ah, no. I'm just trying to find out what's going on." "Well listen, we're opening the Emergency Operating Center tomorrow. Are you interested in working overtime?" "Nah, Ray, I probably won't be back from New York."

So, now we're trying to find a way to the city. Eddy Griff makes a phone call. Gets a hold of somebody from the Coast Guard. Alright, we're going to Bayonne. We've got, thirty guys, forty guys. We shoot over. Mike Nasta is chief of the South Hackensack Fire Department that year. He's got the chief's gig. Okay, following Mike, boom, Seventy-eight, Turnpike. We get to Bayonne. They're not letting anybody off. But we've got the chief's gig and all these cars in tow. Tell the Bayonne cop there, what's going on. We're going to the Coast Guard facility in Bayonne. He jumps in a radio car. We follow him. Well, we pull up to the Coast Guard, not even a base. It's just a station, thirty or forty guys. They got these Coasties standing out there with M-16s and they're young kids. Thank God we had the radio car and the chief's car or we probably could have been shot. As a matter of fact we got Chief Esparolini with us. Lalor gave Nasta the night off because he was supposed to be working. We get there. They know nothing about us coming. Chief Esparolini and I think Nasta go inside. Well, somehow they track us down a boat from the Army Corps of Engineers. It's got a crew of two. It looks like with a full crew it carries six people. Pile all these guys onto this boat. The water was crystal clear. If it was rough we probably would have tipped the boat. We get over to New York and basically we just walked around. Chief Esparolini gets the idea that he's going to go to the Emergency Operations Center and they basically like gave us the bum's rush. What a lot of other guys did was they just didn't listen. They went right to work. We eventually floated around and then we left.

Nasta: I drove a truck. Now I was captain of Five Truck at the time. We were working nights. We were coming in at six o'clock at night. I was delivering a load to Frewsburg. I was hauling containers out of Port Newark. And I go up there. Frewsburg is about a six hour drive. I normally didn't take those kinds of runs when I knew I had to be at work at night, but I took a chance. I get empty at like 7:30 in the morning. My dispatcher is in Port Newark. Pick up the phone, call in, "Listen I'm Empty. I'm on my way back." "Don't come back to the Port." "What are you talking about?" Remember I'm in the truck. I have no news, no nothing. I had nothing to gauge this by. He says, "Don't come back to the Port. The Port's closed." The Port's closed?

Nobody closes Port Newark. He didn't give me much of an explanation. At that point I still did not know what went on. He said, "Something's going on in New York. They closed the ports down."

Okay. So now I'm driving. I said, "I'll stop for breakfast." I'll grab something to eat then I'll continue the rest of the way. So I pull in the truck stop. It's small truck stop. I can't even remember the town in upstate New York. And the television is on. Now I'm sitting there. This is the first I've seen. I'm sitting there having breakfast and I look up. "Holy shit!" This is probably why he told me not to come back to the port. So now cell phones are just starting. I really didn't have a cell phone. I had one of those old cell phones mounted in the tracker trailer I drove, the analog ones.

The funny part was, I belonged to the fire department in South Hackensack as a volunteer. I was the chief that year. So now I start calling my OEM guy in South Hackensack. This guy's a super buff is what we would call him, but he knew everything. His name is Mike Waters. I said, "What the hell is going on?" He said, "Mike just come home. I don't know how you'll get home." He says, "Traffic is a nightmare. People are fleeing the city. They're coming out on foot." I say, "Holy crap." You know. And still all I'd seen was a short report. He says, "Get back." He says, "I'll call you along the way and I'll give you the best route to follow to try to keep you out of the traffic." Okay now I'm in the truck and I'm barreling because now I have two incentives.

This is going on. Mike calls me and tells me South Hackensack is being dispatched to stand by at the George Washington Bridge which they did. So I had that, those people on response, going out. I said, "Oh, shit, I got to get to work." I got to work at six o'clock tonight. I have all these nightmares, visions of I'm not going to get home that quickly or I'm going to be late to work because of the traffic. I just didn't want to be late for work.

So I come out of Frewsburg which is way out in western New York State by the Pennsylvania border, come down through Pennsylvania. There wasn't a soul on the road. As I'm coming down, there was no traffic. I call, "Mike what are you talking about traffic. There's not a car on the road. Everybody must have stayed home." There was no traffic. I cruise right into South Hackensack. I didn't go back to the port. I listened to him. I brought the truck home, to the yard that I rent. Now I rush to the house. My wife is home. She was a stay at home mom at the time, raising our kids, and I'm looking at what happened. It was devastating. And I'm going to be honest with you, I broke down in tears. Because by that time we knew what had happened with the firemen.

This was probably at three o'clock in the afternoon when I got home. And I get in the car. They're probably telling everybody to stay off the roads at that point. So I had the chief's car from South Hackensack which I would never use to go to work in Newark. I always would take my personal vehicle. I say, "You know what? I got to get to work. I'm taking it. It's an official vehicle. Nobody's gonna stop me. So I take that. I get to work and the third tour was working. They were coming off their second day and it's our first night.

Jimmy Weiss tells me, "Mike, guys have gone over there." Frank Bellina and a bunch of other guys have gone over there earlier in the day on their own. Well, in walks and I'll leave the chief un-named, into Five Truck that night. He's going from firehouse to firehouse ordering us not to go, that you would be fired if you go over to New York. So listen, I'm working that night anyway. My responsibility is here. I'm working tonight. With that, the chief who will go nameless, takes off his shirt. He goes, "Now that I delivered the official news, this is what we're doing to get over there." So now there's probably at least two tours working, My guys came in. The third tour is still there. Other guys came in from home. There's quite a few of us in Five Truck. We're going to figure a way to get over there. With that the phone rings. It's my battalion chief, Chief Lalor at the time, so he says, "Listen, Mike, we're going to send people over. I know what the official word is, but we're going to do the right thing. Here's the thing, I want you to put a guy in the seat tonight as acting captain. I want you to go over there." Whatever his reason was. I says, "Alright, no problem." Chief Esparolini comes in the door and he says the same thing, we're going over.

So that became a gathering point. I don't know how many guys we wind up with at Five Truck that night. This is about six, maybe six thirty at night and Esparolini is making some phone calls seeing how we can get over there, transportation. Long story short, somehow we get hooked and we get told to go to the naval base in Bayonne. Report there, they'll get us over there. Okay, so how are we getting there? No official vehicles, so I load guys into the South Hackensack chief's car, guys get in their personal vehicles and off we go. We get to Bayonne. Sure enough, the Coast Guard is waiting. The Coast Guard came. The Coast Guard is waiting for us. They put us on a Coast Guard cutter, right across New York Harbor from Bayonne. Dropped us off at the Battery Yacht Club. So we pull in the Battery Yacht Club. Got off there and you just looked up and I'm sure everybody felt the same way. It was devastation. You literally walked from the water of the Hudson River on a pile of rubble right up to the site. And then we kind of mowed around a little bit because nobody knew.

What we did is we got hooked up with a bunch of guys from Paterson that night. Paterson was told that New York City needed two and a half inch hose. So Paterson showed up in an official Paterson vehicle and stuff with all this two and a half inch hose. All right guys, help them unload the vehicle. Take all the hose, load it onto the Coast Guard cutter. Take it off the Coast Guard cutter. New York was, "Who the hell told you to bring all this?" A bunch of firemen with rolls of two and a half inch hose. We just kind of left it on the docks and went up there.

Rodrigues: I still remember September 11, 2001. I was in Ladder Seven working my first day, ten hour day. So we were going to get off by eighteen hundred hours, six o'clock P.M. Back then Chief Esparolini was a battalion chief. He actually made phone calls to every firehouse looking for volunteers to go and help. So that's why. Deblin Rodrigues has to be there. So I said, yes, if you're going to go. He organized everything so well. He put I believe sixty-five guys together and then he sent a van to pick everybody up. And back then the mayor didn't agree with this. He said, whoever wanted to go there was going to be put on charges. We still went. It's a brotherhood. So he told all of us not to wear our station uniforms which a lot of us didn't do it. We just went with the blue pants and the blue shirt, but we took our bunker gear. We met at Liberty Park. And then the Coast Guard went over to Liberty Park and picked us up and we went over there on a boat.

Ramos: We were working that day. The third tour was working the day of the World Trade Center. And when it came on television, of course everybody was upset, mad, ready to go, ready to fight. At that time we had tens and fourteens. So at the end of the shift of my tour, six o'clock, we all rallied up at Five Truck and Twelve Engine. There were about fifty-eight of us. We rallied up and we're deciding what we're going to do. How we're going to get there? What's going to happen? We were waiting for the powers that be to say something and nothing was coming down. Nothing was coming down from the powers that be, so we just had to go by ourselves. It was Chief Esparolini who was with us at that point in time. And he goes, "If we go we can't have anything that has Newark on it." So we had to take our Newark stuff off because they said if you go over there you're on your own basically.

So we got to the Coast Guard. It was as though we were about to hit the beach. As a Marine, that's what it felt like to me. And the silhouette of New York is dark, the smoke, you see it and then you see the silhouette of the firemen. When we get there it's chaos. They weren't organized yet. They were still waiting on the proper personnel to come in. That's what they needed. Esparolini went and spoke to their commander. They told us to sit down and wait for a while. So as we're waiting you see this crane, big crane comes out with at least a hundred, a hundred and fifty, two hundred men hanging on it, iron workers. They're trying to get to the site. Like I said, without the iron workers it wouldn't have been done. We didn't get to work that night because I guess they weren't ready and they didn't want to put us in danger.

DeCeuster: The day of 9/11, we were working, the third tour was working. I was at One Truck. We're down at the Training Academy. We walk in and they're watching it on TV. You could see it from the Academy, but it was a lot clearer with the cameras for the TV. So the one kid goes, "Come on we got another TV back here." Once we went into the other room the second aircraft hit.

We're like, "Oh, shit." They cancelled everything at the Academy and we went back to quarters. We're biting to the bit here, chomping at the bit. We never got anything. People are getting pissed. That evening I got held over. Now I'm thinking I'm going over there. I'm wanting to go and I had some words with one of the chiefs because I wasn't going there. We wound up setting up a decon over at University Hospital.

Daly: When we grew up, they made a weird TV show, The Twilight Zone. It was like that. The Twilight Zone, weird as all hell. Felt like I was on another planet. Other guys were laughing and joking. I was like dead serious. Billy Melodic was with me. Me and Billy were together. I had taken a camera with me. And I took pictures as we were going over in the Coast Guard cutter. There were fifty of us. When I got over there, I threw the camera away. The other guys were taking pictures. I slapped it out of their hands. I said, no, no, no.

Arce: I was watching the first plane strike one of the buildings. I was at my mother's house, fifteen story apartment. I saw the second plane hit as it came. I knew Newark was going to go because I heard that some of the guys were interested in going. So I went to the firehouse and I heard everybody was leaving. At the firehouses, we all got together, about thirty-five of us. We ended up down in the port where we were shipped over that same afternoon by a boat. They parked right in front of the collapse.

Johnson: Actually I was off. I just got off that morning and I was taking my son, he was about four years old, I was taking him to school and was helping at school. I saw a plane crash into the building. I'm looking at it and it got to the point where it was like mass chaos. I went down to the firehouse to see what they were going to do. Are you having guys going over to New York? And they said yes, so we took a ferry over. Captain Volkert was my captain and his daughter was at Pace University. It was almost like a mission of Saving Private Ryan.

Tarantino: I was off. I was on the second tour working at Eleven Truck on Ninth Street. I used to drive a truck delivering orange juice. When the World Trade Center got hit, obviously I'm in the truck. I'm listening on the radio and you hear the whole thing. Well, when the second tower got hit, I realized it's something bad. My daughter was real young at the time. I guess she was two, two and a half years old. She was in daycare in Livingston. So I call up my boss, I said, "Listen, I'm going to get my daughter. I don't know what craziness is going on." I was supposed to work that night. We were working nights. We were still on tens and fourteens. So I was working that night. I went and got my daughter and I came into work early. I think I came into work about four o'clock. And I remember Eddie Griff was coming in and he was making phone calls. He knew someone with the Coast Guard, got him over there.

At the time they didn't want anybody to go. And my wife said, "Listen, you're going to get into trouble." I mean it was pretty clear they didn't want anybody going over there. But the next morning we set up that we were going to go anyway later in the day because all the guys that went that night and the guys that went that morning said that you have to wait in this long fucking line to get in. Now when I first started the fire department, after a couple of years I went to work on Wall Street. I worked at Forty Fulton. I used to come out of World Trade Center Five and walk right down Fulton Street. So I know the streets really well. When we were deciding to go, we went out at about three, four o'clock in the afternoon , I guess on the next day, on the Wednesday.

Charlie Krutulis was my captain. He had just retired a couple of months before. He was like, "You've got to wait for me to get there." We took a caravan of about maybe six cars. We left from Ninth Street. I had heard you have to have all your stuff with you or they're not letting you through. You've got to have ID., the whole thing. So we go on the Turnpike. The Turnpike is completely empty. It was the most eerie thing ever. We get stopped by this military guy in the front and he checks everybody's IDs. Let's us go through and I'll never forget. They had to move a tank out of the way of the Holland Tunnel. There was a tank that was going across the Holland Tunnel. They moved the tank and we went through. So now I'm sitting there and I'm going, "There's no way I'm going to stand in this fucking line. There's no way I'm going to deal with that on West. I think it was on West, where the line was. It was basically going down to the Empire State Building. There's no way I'm going there.

When we came out of the tunnel on the opposite side, again they ask you for ID., the whole thing. So he starts to point. Now I've been to New York five million times. I'm like, "No." I made up this story. That I know this chief and he's got to meet us on this certain street. I don't know what street name I said. He radioed into somebody. I just picked the right street. There was a staging area on that street. Liberty I think it was. There was a staging area on Liberty. I said, "I'm supposed to meet him on Liberty, across from Century Twenty-one."

Which is where I used to come out from the World Trade Center Five. It just so happened, they were clearing that street. If we would have gotten there maybe six hours earlier, we wouldn't have been able to get through because that street was still filled with debris. They had cleared that street. So we were able to divert and go through down a one way the wrong way. And we literally parked right next to the World Trade Center. I think we had six cars. We put labels on it so they wouldn't pick them up and tow them. So, instead of getting staged and told where to go, we walked on the back side. If you're at World Trade Center Five, you're all the way at the opposite end of the corner of World Trade Center One and World Trade Center Two is to your right. Ten Engine was across the street from World Trade Center One. We were on the opposite side. We walked down and then made the right at Ten Engine and then just literally walked up on the pile. It worked out to be amazing.

Sorace: Around 1996, fire departments in the state like Elizabeth, Jersey City, Atlantic City, they were all trying to start this new thing called urban search and rescue. So, Jersey City, Elizabeth, and Atlantic City among the few, a lot of their chiefs got involved and they were starting this state urban search and rescue team. Newark had been asked to get involved with it. They were involved with it a little bit, doing the investigative stuff. I remember going over to our academy here with Chief Langenbach. A notice came out. Anybody want to get involved with this urban search and rescue thing? Newark's going to start their own. I went down there one early evening and Chief Langenbach took a bunch of notes. He wanted to know some of your qualifications. Where ever this list was going, I don't know. So it ended up the state starts this urban search and rescue team. Newark's not included in it. It's like Elizabeth, Jersey City and whatever. So in 2000, I ended up getting an application for it. I filled out the application and I have to send it through the law department of Newark. It's basically a memorandum of understanding. They sign off on this agreement to allow me to be a member of this State Police urban search and rescue team. So I got on the team in 2000 and I had to do a lot of training. You get them all while you're on the team. So shortly after I was on the team, we ended up being deployed to 9/11. OEM, New Jersey State Police, runs the team. So we get deployed to 9/11. We were, I guess you would say, the second responders. We were the first mutual aid that New York City called for the incident. As soon as the call was made, we had our advanced support team shoot out there and size up or whatever. Meanwhile our whole rest of the team is being mustered. We deployed out of Lakehurst, what was then "Naval Base." Now it's "Joint Base." We have all our trucks, all of our apparatus, and offices down there. So, being that I was on the team, I go down there, get all our stuff together, and we get deployed. We're on the scene over in New York and we split up, we set up, get deployed there. When we go to someplace like there, we set up our own base camp, our own facilities. We don't have to go there and say, "Oh, New York we need water. New York we need food. New York we need a tent." We come there and everything is self-supportive. We're there for ten days. We work twelve hour shifts, usually seven in the morning to seven at night and then we rotate. We can have several different squads of people working at a time. Usually it's groups of rescue crews; it can be six guys. And each rescue crew will have a haz-mat guy, an EMS guy, search people, canine. We can divide up where ever needed.

Perdon: I went over there with the guys from Ten Engine. It was myself, Danny Farrell, Paul Bartelloni, and two guys from the first tour from Ten Engine, John Nepa and Jimmy Lynn. So we all go over. It was funny getting there. We jump in Nepa's Expedition. So, we're heading over. We go through the tunnel. We get stopped going in. We tin them. We get stopped going out of the tunnel. We tin them. This was then at that point where they wanted everybody to go to a central location and then they would assign you if they were ever going to assign you. Well, we get out of the tunnel and a cop calls down and says, "Hey, we've got some firemen here." They said, "Bring them right to ground zero." So, we parked the car. They drove us right to ground zero. Everybody else had to go to the central location. We kind of lucked out from the whole get-go.

Farrell: We worked that night because were still doing tens and fourteens. And the first thing I remember is trying to reach out to a good buddy of mine who worked on the sixtieth floor of the second Trade Center that got hit. It got hit on the eightieth floor so it got hit above him. He's the first person I thought of. I tried to call him. And he didn't answer his phone. I called his house phone. I said, "Listen

I'm leaving you a message. Call me as soon as you get this. Let me know you're okay." Long story short, I heard from him the next day. But we went over the next morning, George Perdon, Pauly Bartelloni, John Nepa God rest his soul, and Jimmy Lynn.

Bartelloni: I was at Ten Engine. That's where I spent most of my career. Everybody was chomping at the bit to get out there. So we went in to work the night shift and then between our nights we went. We took a car out there. They met us at the tunnel. They realized we were firemen with our turnout gear and everything and they escorted us in. We went to the pile.

Brownlee: I didn't go the first day. In fact I was in my living room ironing clothes when I saw it on TV. As soon as I saw it, I went downstairs, threw some stuff in the car and went to leave. The lady across the street came out and said, "You see what's happening over in New York?" I said, "Yeah, I'm on my way up there now. There's got to be five hundred firemen dead." I got in the car and it took me forty-five minutes to get from here to the firehouse. (normally a 90 minute commute) I didn't leave that day. I worked that night. I went the next day. Wednesday, Thursday, and Friday I was over there.

A couple of us went in my car; put all the stuff in the trunk. We went to the Holland Tunnel. The cops stop you and they look in the car. They see the firemen, go. And we went. We didn't have to pay any tolls or anything. We worked the pile those three days.

Partridge: When the attack took place on September eleventh I was up on Cape Cod. We had a family house on Cape Cod for many years. It was actually my second home. It might have been home more than New Jersey actually, but I was up there. We had a huge picture window in the front with a sofa under it. I loved to just lie on that sofa and read. And I was laying on that sofa reading and my parents were in the next room which was kind of like a den slash TV room. And they called me in and said, "Pete there's a huge fire at the World Trade Center. It seems like a plane might have hit the building." So I ran in to look and like everybody else, you know, my first thought was, "Oh, a private somehow must have hit." When I saw the magnitude of it on TV, I knew it was a major crisis. My father was asking me my opinion. Can they put this fire out? So we were talking about that and then the second plane hit. At which point everybody knew it was a terror attack. I remember the first thing I thought and the first thing I said out loud when the buildings actually collapsed. I said, "Well we just watched them kill three hundred firemen." Now that was my first reaction and it turned out I wasn't too far off the mark.

I was frantic to get back. I called my sister, who's heavily involved in the world of EMS. She was already on the road. Her unit had already been dispatched down to Jersey City to be part of a triage station at Liberty State Park. But I got her on the phone which was lucky because a lot of cell phone communications were down at the time. I got her and she said don't even try to come home. Everything's closed. You cannot get here. All bridges, all highways leading to New York are closed. If you try to come home, you're going to have to swing out through Ohio and Pennsylvania to get there. I said, okay. It was a horrible day for me because I was stuck up on the Cape. I felt completely helpless.

I was always a big FDNY buff. I had a lot of friends over there. I knew some of them were going to be dead. I didn't know who or how many. I was trying to get people on the phone. Naturally I couldn't. Half the time calls weren't even going through and when they were they weren't being answered. I finally got one guy's wife on the phone. And she said, "Bobby's okay. I do know that, but I also don't know anything further. I know it's real bad. I know it's very, very bad. But that's all I know. Right now I know Bobby's okay." So, that was about it for hours and hours. I was just glued to the TV. Couldn't get home. And then at some point late at night, the guy Bobby whose wife I had spoken to gave me a call. He started naming names of guys that were lost and I did know a lot of them. It turns out when all was said and done, I knew seventeen guys from the FDNY that had been lost. Some of them were acquaintances and some of them were pretty good friends.

I went home the next day because by that time they had opened up things to the extent that I would have been able to get across the Tappan Zee Bridge. So I went home that way. I got home I guess late in the afternoon or the early evening. Went down to the firehouse in Newark and there were guys going over. We went over.

The first time we went over there, I think we had Steve LaPenta's pickup truck. Nobody stopped us. At that point the tunnels and bridges were still closed into Manhattan, but we were obviously a truck load of firefighters with turnout gear and equipment and everything like that. Anytime we got to a check point, we just got waved right through. We would park at Eight Truck in lower Manhattan which is kind of like down by Tribeca area. Most of the time we were able to hitch a ride on some kind of vehicle that was going down to the site. I think maybe once or twice we had to walk, but in most cases there was always somebody going back or forth that you could jump on with. We spent a lot of time there. Whenever we weren't working in the firehouse we were kind of pretty much over in the city for about two weeks I guess.

McGovern: I was amazed, you know, at the outpouring of the guys from Newark that went over there on their own time after being told that they could be punished for it. Which was a big mistake for the city, should have never happened. They should have immediately sent at least a Signal Nine there when it happened. Right after it happened I called the fire chief; is there a recall? I couldn't believe, no. And then they specifically ordered, I want nobody going over there. That pissed me off.

Two days after it happened, the thirteenth of September, we were sent there. I called Chief Jones. I said, "You got to send me over there." About a half hour passed and he called back. He said, "Yeah go ahead." He sent us, a signal nine. So, it was frustrating.

I was sent there as a task force leader. There were roughly eight to ten of us, Seven Engine, Eleven Truck. We went over on the rigs.

They sent us to Brooklyn first. We were covering a firehouse in Brooklyn for about an hour, two hours. Then they dispatched us to the World Trade Center where we parked the rigs and went to work.

Jackson: We actually got dispatched over there, Engine Seven and Truck Eleven and Battalion One, Chief McGovern. Not the day of 9/11. We weren't working, but I think the next day we went over there. We spent the whole day over there. First we went to Staten Island. And the company there, they lost the whole company and it was a change of tour too. They actually brought the rescue rig back. It was a rescue company and an engine company house. The engine company didn't come back, but they brought the rescue company back. The whole one side of it, man, it was like somebody just took a shotgun to it and just went down it and just blasted. The paint and everything was just sheared off it. And the other side had nothing wrong with it.

We stayed there. We have New York standard hydrants, so we were able to fit their threads with our feed lines and everything. And we went on a couple of runs over there with a guide. Then they sent us to Brooklyn. They had an engine company and then they had like an ice melt company or whatever. It was almost like a salvage company in Newark. There were a couple of guys there. They were like, old timers. We never even went on a run there. It was actually Bensonhurst that we went to and I think it was maybe a slower area because we really didn't get that many runs. Then they called us to come down to Ground Zero. We went there probably from like one o'clock until like five o'clock. Because we had to get back at eighteen hundred hours for the change of tours.

Greene: Yes. I came in one morning, I can't recall exactly how many days after the attack and the towers came down. I'd have to go look in the journal. It could have been two, three days or whatever. I came in that morning and Chief McGovern said that we were going to the World Trade Center. I was the acting captain at Engine Seven. It was myself, Orlando Arce, Rufus Jackson and probably someone else. I can't recall who it was though. Maybe it was Danny Snyder, I'm not sure. But at any rate it was Chief McGovern, Engine Seven, and Ladder Eleven that went. We proceeded on the road and somehow we were detoured through a Rescue Squad on Staten Island. And we were just kind of like standing by there, back filling because all their people went to the World Trade Center for the recovery, rescue and recovery. We were there a couple hours. There were a good number of companies there. Then the Deputy Chief came, talked to Chief McGovern and requested that we go to Brooklyn. I believe Ladder Eleven stayed on Staten Island. Engine Seven went to Bensonhurst, Brooklyn. We were there a couple more hours. I can't recall if we responded to a call there or not. If it was, it was very minor in nature. From there they directed us to the World Trade Center.

Montalvo: On 9/11, I was actually in the Essex County Court House going for my divorce. I remember I was out there early in the morning. We were there like eight o'clock in the morning and all I remember was sitting outside, all of the sudden all the Sheriff's officers that were outside in the hallway, they had all gone inside. All the civilians were outside. I'm with the civilians, we're out there. I'm like what the hell is going on? Suddenly somebody came out and said, "A plane just flew into the World Trade Center, little while later another plane. Now they're getting ready to shut down the courthouse. So they said, "With what happened today, we're shutting down the courthouse." All I remember was coming down stairs. I told my ex-wife, "Go home, get the kids and go home. I don't know what's going on, but you know what? It doesn't sound good. Get the kids, go home."

I wound up driving from the Essex County Courthouse to Bergen and Lehigh. Took me an hour to get from Market and Springfield to Bergen and Lehigh. Took me an hour. I kept watching the rest of the day just unfold on TV over there. Guys were calling in. Guys were driving in. Oh my God. What's the whole thing going on? I couldn't even go home that day because Market Street was pretty much shut down. Back then I lived over on Foundry Street and apparently the street was shut down and you couldn't go anywhere in the city. So I kind of just stayed at the firehouse that night.

The city didn't want us to go. . Actually we were told that if we went over there we would be in trouble. The mayor's office put something out, a memo out or something. No on duty personnel are to be going over there, but we were off duty. I think that's how we got around it. Well, we're not on duty. We're going on our own time.

We're not doing it on city time. They lost three hundred and forty three guys.

Next morning our shift was working the day shift tens and fourteens. So what we did was we did our day shift. The other crew came in early, about four-thirty because they heard what was going on and they called us and said, "You guys going down there?" We told them yeah, so they came in. At five o'clock we all jumped in my van and we drove into New York City.

We all went in our bunker gear. They told us when we're traveling to make sure we have our driver's license and our fire department ID. So that's what we did. We got to the tunnels and everything had to be inspected. We all had to get out of the car. They had to check all of our equipment. They checked us. They waved us through. They took us over there. Wound up getting into ground zero. It had to be I want to say about six thirty, seven. Got over there and we were supposed to go see the command post because they had two, three command posts set up at the time. The furthest command post where we started out was for all the volunteer towns that were coming in. They were putting all the guys over there. All the paid departments they were sending them over to another command post so we went over there. We go in and help the guys there. We just started digging. We spent the night just digging over there, helping the guys dig. We came back to Newark; worked our next shift; and by that time we had started working on a bus for the next day. We knew we were going to be off the next day. So what we did was we hired a bus company to drive us into New York City the Friday after. The bus company came in, picked us up, and we went in there.

Castelluccio: I was actually working at Ronnie Coco's house. He had just bought a house and we were building this big addition onto his house. He was building a house attached to his house. I was framing his house for him. And his wife says, "A plane just flew into the World Trade Center." I'm saying, "Well that's odd." It was crystal blue out. I'm like, "What kind of plane? A small plane? What?" She's not really sure. So got down off of framing the second floor and we're sitting in the living room. We're watching it on TV. Then we saw the second plane go into it. I was working that night. We were still on the ten fourteens. I had to go into work that night. My first reaction was I called my wife up. I told her to get the kids out of school. I told her to go to the bank and get as much money as we have in the bank out of the bank. And she's like, "What's going on?" I says, "Just do what I'm telling you. Get as much money as you could and get the kids out of the school." Because by then you knew we were under attack. I told her, "I'm going into work. I'm probably not going to see you for a while." I didn't want to get her too worried, but we worked that night. Had to go in. Pretty much watched everything on TV. You could see the smoke from Avon Avenue.

Next day we all got into a truck and we drove. We went there, came back, went to work, went back again. We went through the Lincoln Tunnel. The cops knew we were firemen. We all had our gear, our IDs. They were cool. They weren't supposed to, but they let us go. They knew we were there to go and help. After about the fourth day, they got really, really tight with security and bringing people in.

Masters: We had two large trucks. Charlie Krutulis had a big truck. He fit maybe four guys in. Another guy, four guys with his truck. We threw all the gear in the back and drove in. So that's how we got there. We had no problems getting in there. But for the first few nights like when it actually happened and then the first few nights afterwards, everybody just bombarded them. They were grateful. It was chaos, but then again it wasn't.

Sperli: We went for two days. One was I think the second day after it happened. That would be like the thirteenth and I think the fifteenth we went. It was surreal. I remember driving into it and we had to show ID, fireman's ID, and we had all our gear in the car. There were like four of us, five of us, and the cops would check the ID and then they waved us in. It was just so quiet. It was like a ghost town. You didn't see anybody walking around. Then you started walking down slowly. You heard this noise like the rumble of the tractors. When you got there you saw all the iron workers cutting the beams with torches, see all the sparks and everything. You could still see the smoke billowing up, see that skeleton of what was left of the World Trade Center. It was just a very mixed emotional moment, you know.

Griggs: I went over there one day on a Thursday morning after we got relieved. We drove in. I was with Sal Bidot, Chief Donnelly, Tommy Mastroeni, Andrew Crowley down at Ladder Four on this tour. We drove in and we worked a day and then we drove back out. I don't remember whether we went via the Holland Tunnel or the Lincoln Tunnel though. But all we had to do was flip our IDs and they let us in. But then shortly after that they stopped it because there was just no accountability. I mean you saw firemen from Sacramento, Chicago. There was just too any people all over the place.

Lee: Yes, I went over to the World Trade Center. I think it was two days after or three days after. It was me, Captain Otis Johnson, Ray Hatton. It was a bunch of us. We just jumped in the back of Otis' pickup and we all just went straight over the tunnel. At that time there was a very minimum that you could do.

Ostertag: I went. It happened on a Tuesday. That was our first night in, Tuesday-Wednesday. So we went that Thursday. I went down with Mike Nasta, Kevin Mitchko, Artie Davis, a bunch of guys from Five Truck. That's the day we went there. I was only there for a day.

Pierre: The day of the airplane I was working. In fact we were watching it on TV. I was like, "Oh my God. Is this right? Is this true? What is going on here?" The second plane went into the building we went, "Oh my God. This is serious." But I was on duty so I didn't have a chance to go that day. Two days later we went to the World Trade Center.

Meier: I went. The day of the Trade Center, I was home and I went to the bagel store, looked at the TV, saw it on TV, and wound up going home. See my wife and I just had a new born. I wound up calling to the firehouse, expecting at any time that they were going to do a recall, which they never did. And when I finally got through to somebody at the firehouse they said, we're going to University Hospital to set up the decon for any victims that come over. But you're more than welcome to come up because the guys that are finished with the shift at six o'clock were going to go into the city. You could work as a swap or you could go into the city. By the time I got up to Newark, the guys already left. It was such a tremendous catastrophe. Everybody was unsure of what was going on. I didn't want to go in by myself. I would rather go in with a group. We were all unclear of what was happening. So I wound up going back home and then the way the shifts fell, my two ten hour days fell the next two days. So it happened on a Tuesday, so Wednesday and Thursday were my two ten hour days and most of the guys that were going in the city were just going in during the day. So Friday there was a collection. I think we met at the Squad, Mulberry and Lafayette at I think five o'clock in the morning and we went in.

Burkhardt: I was in the firehouse. I was the acting Chief the day that the plane hit. We just came back from a fire down below on

Sherman Avenue. I was riding an exercise bike and when the second plane hit I jumped off the bike; I got dressed; I knew there was something happening.

When the first building dropped, I'll tell you what, I never had a feeling like that in my life, never imagined it. I figured like the top twenty floors would go. Never expected that thing to drop floor by floor by floor. And then the second one went. I said, "Jeez, you know, that was amazing to see it." Later on that afternoon, I had a couple of runs. I had a haz-mat and I was riding through the city. I went downtown and there were cops on every corner, by the Gateway, the FBI. You've got government offices there. The phone company, I was up and down Broad Street, riding around just checking the city out. There were cops all over the place. I look at the news at noon. There are people leaving Newark Airport like they were leaving Vietnam. The fire department didn't call in one person. The cops mobilized everybody. I'm down at Five Truck. They're sending guys over. Guys are screaming at me. Get people, get a truck, get us porta-lights. Porta-lights? You can't get a porta-light for the firehouse, now you want me to get you an engine?

They say, "You going with us?" I say, "No. I'm acting chief, how can I go with you?" Frank Bellina came in with cases of water. I mean these guys mobilized a small soup kitchen in a matter of like an hour and a half and they were ready to go. If somebody robs a bank, nobody's lining up to get their guns and go charge a bank, but there's something about fires. Everybody thinks they can do it. To see guys mobilize that quickly to go over there and we don't even know whether the worst is over. Because it's still in it's infancy at the time, the attacks. We didn't know. And yet guys are ready to go over there. They didn't give a shit how they're getting there. Boat, plane, train, they didn't care. They just wanted to go.

The day we did go, a Port Authority cop climbed into the truck with us, checked our IDs. We're in uniform, had our gear. He held your ID card right up to you. When you go through that Holland Tunnel, you'd be the only truck in that tunnel, the only vehicle. You knew there was something going on. Then I walked down the Westside Highway and to hear people cheering, I mean that's nice, but it's also chilling that something like that happened. To come out of there with three hundred and forty three guys to lose, I think it was a miracle it was that low. But to see it. Read the papers. I just couldn't fathom something like that. Never expected that. And then the second one dropped, just unbelievable.

LaPenta: I didn't hear any PASS alarms (personal alarm safety system, a small devise that sounds an alarm when a firefighter stops moving for 30 seconds). I think I was so fixated on no sound that I didn't recognize any other sound that was going on around me. Not one of us really said a word the whole time. We were just walking down the street and I think we were just taking it in. Then we come around the corner and you're really starting to see. We were three, four, five blocks away. Now we have to climb over debris to even get to where we had to go which is bizarre. It was just such a surreal scene. It was like a disaster movie, an end of the world type of disaster film. When you get closer and closer then you really start taking in the devastation. I mean the fire department was decimated. I mean they were gone. There was nothing.

As we got closer to the scene, you could see there was no equipment. There was no apparatus. It was just completely destroyed. Other buildings were coming down around us. We were working. We were crawling in. I went up to a battalion chief. I said, "Well, what do I tell this guy?" The guys all turned to me and said, "Hey man, you're on the captain's list. You're getting promoted soon. Tell him you're a captain and take it from there." I said, okay. So I went up to a battalion chief. I said, "Chief, Steve LaPenta I'm a captain in the Newark Fire Department rescue company." He looked at me. He goes, "You have your equipment?" I said, "I have some equipment.

The rig, I'm not a hundred percent sure what's going on with the apparatus, but we're here. We all have the same stuff." He said, "If you could find what's left, take your crew and go down and see so and so, you can't miss him. Tell him you're a rescue company. They got something going on. Go over there." I said, "Okay."

So that's what we did. We went around. I asked for the guy. I don't remember the guy's name. I think it was like Blair or something. And he says, "Yeah, up here." When I got to the top of the pile, this chief was arguing with a police officer, an ESP cop. "No, that's our guy down there. We're going to go get him." And the chief was like, "Listen, you guys don't do this. We do. We'll get him out." Urrr. This chief looked at me and goes, "Who are you?" Because at the time, believe it or not, we had a retired New York City firefighter from Rescue Two or Three working for a turnout gear manufacturer and they gave us all this gear to try out. It was identical to the stuff that they were wearing in New York. So our coats said Rescue One on them. We looked like New York City firemen. He looked at me up and down. I said, "I'm a captain in Rescue in the city of Newark." He said, "Alright, supposedly we have a guy trapped in this hole. We got to get down there, this and that." And the cop goes, "Why are you letting these guys in the hole?" The chief turned to him and says, "These are the most trained guys we got right now. Get in the fucking hole kid." Just like that. Let's go. And we went in the hole. You know, I mean there were a lot more four letter words thrown out that night, but I'm trying to be polite. That's what we did. It was unbelievable.

I knew a lot of guys from over there. Pete Partridge was my captain at the time. You know Pete knew everybody over there. So he wasn't with us. I think Pete was up on the Cape. Pete was on vacation. He was up in Cape Cod I think at the time. So we were there that night without a boss. But we went back for a week or so. We were there for like a week. Back and forth going and you know the sad thing was I think we all had hope that we were going to get somebody. You figured this is a hundred and ten story building. Every floor is the size of an acre. There's got to be somebody here. We have to find somebody, right? And we never found anybody. The whole time I was there, we didn't find a whole person. We found pieces. We found the remains, but we never found an intact individual. But then after stepping back and looking at this scene three or four days later in the daylight, it's impossible. I mean the vast area of the destruction. It was just incredible.

I remember too that night we were going into the hole and working and working. You can't see. You couldn't see anything. We took porta-lights from the rig, We took everything off the rig. A couple of guys started screaming, "The building, the building's gonna fall. Run, run, run." And I'm like, "Where are we going to run to?" Seriously, where are you running to? We're twenty stories high on a pile of rubble. Where are you running to? You're in the center of an acre. How fast can you run over debris? I've had a lot of hairy moments on this job, but that was one of the times where I really thought it was over. I was with Dagna. I said, "We ain't going home." Shit was just coming down around us and we couldn't see. I literally just put my hands on my head and was just waiting for it, waiting for it, and it never happened. That's when number Seven came on us and it was unbelievable.

You know we never found office equipment. There were no printers, desks, computers, nothing, but yet you would dig and you would find a pair of eyeglasses that had not a scratch on them. The whole area where we were digging for five hours, you find nothing and then you get a pair of reading glasses. The dogs were there, the search and rescue dogs and they were getting hits everywhere. The dog would get a hit over here and we'd dig and it's nothing. I guess the scent was just so overwhelming.

Then one afternoon, Pete and I were taking a blow and we were sitting on this I-beam and I looked and I said, "Pete what is that?" He said, "Where?" I said, "That piece of steel. What is that?" And it was the aerial ladder. It was the joint where the base of the rung tied into the base of the turntable. It wound up it was Ten Truck. Their firehouse was right at the base, Ten Engine/Ten Truck was right there. So then we go, "Hey we got a rig here." Everybody swarmed on the rig. We dug until our fingers bled. Nothing, nothing. Maybe they were underneath or in the cab but I mean this truck was just destroyed.

Langenbach: For the ten days we went there, we would meet in Newark and then caravan over. Same thing, go the same way. Same thing, down Two-Eighty, through the Holland Tunnel and into the city and go to the same place. When they shut the site down or locked it down, then it was just a question of going through their security to get into the site to work. They never stopped us. In fact that original crew did ten days and then we sent another crew over. John Wheeler with the second crew and they were over another ten days. Yeah, they never impeded that. Then some of us went to Fresh Kills. That's where all the debris was going, to Fresh Kills. They went to do the same thing that we were doing at the pile. Except now a little more controlled looking through for evidence or whatever.

We worked out of the Burger King on the corner. The Trade Center complex is here and just south of that on the next corner down is a Burger King. There was a lot of damage to the building, but somebody spray painted on the side, NYPD headquarters. So that's where we worked, on the second floor of that. We worked out of there, the second floor of that building. We worked with the NYPD, their Arson/Bomb Squad. The first thing they were doing, they were looking for one of their own people that they lost. That was the first thing, but we ended up going on one corner and as stuff came down, we would just go through it really quickly, just give a look at it to see if there's anything there that we can identify. And then they finally said, "Well, this is pointless." Now they're bringing in cranes and shovels and everything to get all this stuff. We spent the rest of that first day and then every day for the next ten days just on the pile. Just working the pile alongside these guys, these NYPD guys.

Being explosive investigators allegedly or supposedly or at least trained that way, we're looking for some kind of evidence. But then looking at the size of the pile and the amount of things, this is an impossible task. That's finding a needle in you know ten thousand haystacks. You're never going to find anything. But that came down later. It was just like everybody else, stand in a line and pass stuff out. pass stuff back and forth and go from different sides of the pile. We found some things, like that first day, finding things that were from the Windows on the World and a human finger. Because I guess that would be the top of the pile. It's kind of sad. Everybody's thinking the same thing. There's got to be a void with people in it somewhere. Turned out to not be the case.

Every day we worked someplace else, but always with those same guys. Show up in the morning, we'd get there at like seven in the morning and work until it got dark and then leave. And go back and do the same thing the next morning. On the first Sunday we were there, it's like a routine now. Just go show up at whatever corner of the pile you're going to work from. You're going to work there. We're standing, passing stuff back and forth and all of the sudden you see there's less people. You're looking around and there're less and less people. There was a Catholic priest or he was a Brother. He's doing communion up on the pile. So people just sort of drift over, take their communion, and go back to work again. It was just amazing. And the other thing that really still stays with me is one of the days, I think it was a Thursday, maybe, the first Thursday. We're walking out and there's all these people holding candles. They're singing God Bless America. I couldn't believe it. When I get home, my little street, people are out in the street with candles. It was just the most amazing thing.

But yeah it was something. And another thing, these restaurants all in down there would make these magnificent meals and just walk around and hand them out to you. You'd be sitting, you know, sitting on the curb somewhere and take a break and somebody'd come up and say, "You guys hungry yet?" Some four star restaurant would come by and drop off a meal. But it was just amazing. It was amazing to see how all those people come together like that. There was a whole like tool bin. It was gigantic. All our tools that were donated, all went to this place. If you needed an ax you went in there and got an ax. If you needed a shovel, you went in there and got a shovel. It was amazing. I was back in the city in the Arson Squad after I did my ten days and I get a phone call. They routed it to me for some reason and it was a guy from Texas. He says, "I've got five tractor-trailer loads of water. Where do you want it?" I don't know. We sent him off somewhere. Everybody wanted to do something, everybody.

Another cool thing, you think about these things. It's on like the third or fourth day, I get back home and I go to the Arson Squad. I'm done. Before I go home and I get a call from the Director. "The Mayor wants to see you." Yeah, this could be really, really good or really, really bad. So Chief Jones drives me down there. Just me and the Director, we're going to meet with the Mayor, sit down with him. He goes, "What's going on? What did you do? How are things?" And he says, "Did you talk to Mayor Giuliani?" I said, "No." I'm kind of like down a little further. He said, "I want to call him. What should I do?" And I said, "If it was me I would say, 'I'm here. Whatever you need, I'll send it to you.' But that's the best you can do, offer it to him. I'll never forget that.

Bellina: When we get there and we don't know what to do. There's nothing to do. We're floundering around. I'll never forget the chirp of all these PASS alarms going on. Where we were at was right by the World Financial Center where there was like a tube at the Gateway building that connected that to the Trade Center. That was collapsed on an ambulance and that was the command post. When I looked down they had all stuff stored there. They were all gone. The command post was gone, the tactical command post. So we got involved with stretching some hose and seeing these guys come out. They were covered in dust and the chirping of the alarms, it was unbelievable.

We were there when Tower Seven came down. We were actually in Ground Zero when Tower Seven fell. They came over the loudspeakers on the rigs or whatever. Everybody get out of the way. They knew it was coming down. We were in no jeopardy, but we were there when Tower Seven came down. We actually accomplished nothing, but there was really nothing to do. We never saw anything like that before. There was nothing left. There was nowhere to reach. We were finding fragments of a jaw bone and it was almost dried. It was almost like it was in a museum. That's the kind of stuff we were finding and there was really nothing for us to do. So we leave. We worked there until eight o'clock.

From there we get sent to an island close to Ellis Island where they set up a very big, elaborate decon set up. And we were deconned. We were hosed off. Then there were tons of ambulances over there from the State of New Jersey. An ambulance brought us back to New Jersey, maybe two or three.

With that devastation, I didn't think we were going to go back. The Director was really hot. He didn't know we went, but you're not going back. We weren't paying attention to it. Then I get a phone call from John Agoston saying we got to go back. And I'm saying, John, I mean, we were there. I said, "John, we did nothing the first day." I mean, what can we do? He says "Listen, they're organizing things over there. We got to go back." I said, "Okay." I told my wife I was going back. John Wilson had a father-in-law that was a chief in the New York City fire department, retired. John Wilson says, "My father-in-law's going to go back with us. He's a retired New York City fireman." I didn't think anything of it. At this time we took our own vehicles to Liberty State Park again. We get out of the vehicle and I meet John Wilson's father-in-law. The guy had to be seventy years old. He looked frail. He had a helmet on, a leather helmet that was from 1970. He had a rubber coat on that was down to his knees. I'm feeling embarrassed at the moment that this is the New York City fireman that we're bringing with us. So, we go into the same section we were, into the Financial Building and I'm looking onto this broken glass. I see they look like ants on the pile. There were so many firemen out there with buckets. And I'm going, "Okay, they got something going on here." Like they're organized to an extent.

There's a chief at the door, he goes, "Listen I don't want anybody else out there right now. We appreciate your help, but I'm trying to get control over this." I'm talking hundreds of firefighters out there. People taking pictures. He's trying to get control of this one section that we're in. And out of the back comes John Wilson's father-in-law. He goes, "Let me out here and talk to him." The chief that stopped us had walked into the pile. I see him, John Wilson's father-in-law walk out to the pile with this guy. All of the sudden I see everybody and their mother coming up hugging him. I see that respect that we have. I'm saying, "Oh my God, you idiot. This guy is someone." So all of the sudden he's waving us. Come on in. We break the stalemate again. Go out. I don't know how many of us there are, maybe five or six at this point. We're out on the pile and we work along with a dog. I don't know where the dog was from, but he's a cadaver dog. I don't know how long we worked. We're working this pile and there's a New York City fire department crew. They're trying to find their apparatus and the guys they work with. They're all gone. They're all dead. We're down deep into this pile, maybe four foot down into this little tunnel kind of thing and the dog's there. He takes a hit. The dog's going crazy. So, we locate the body. The body was dismembered and disemboweled. But the one thing about him, we could tell his race. He was black and he had a wedding band on. The New York City firemen were looking down because we found something. And they're like, "Is it one of our guys? Give us something." So we gave them a shoe and they're looking at it. "Nah, he's not a firefighter. He's a civilian." Because he had no clothes on.

His clothes were ripped off the guy. Now we didn't know if the guy was in the building or was he on the street or did he jump or what. We didn't know what it was. So we proceeded to bag this guy and I lost it. I had a mask on, but I was getting sick from the smell and from what we were seeing. I was throwing up. Nothing was coming up, but I had dry heaves. It took a lot to control myself. I'll never forget the New York City firemen looking down when we got the body up and saying, "You guys did a good job." I couldn't believe we were being complimented by a department that took such a large hit. And the one thing about it though, when we pulled this body out, on his chest was a bolt from the building. It was like the head of a bolt that was maybe two inches and the length the bolt was maybe an inch and a half and it was cracked off. It was on his chest. I'll never forget grabbing the bolt and looking at it. John Wilson's father-in-law looked over the edge. He goes, "Take it; put it in your pocket. You build something around that bolt." I was going to take it, but I felt it was disgusting taking it like it's a souvenir. When he said that to me, I put it in my pocket. Never thought anything of it. So we get the body out and we do other things there, but that was like enough for me. I said, "I'm not coming back here. They don't need us. They're organizing things. They don't need us," We all agreed that we're not coming back. We felt good about it. I always wanted to look up, who it could have possibly been. Because it was one of the first identifiable bodies. But I never really went that far. I always wanted to do it. I probably wouldn't know how to do it, but I always wanted to know what it was about. I can picture his ring in my head to this day.

Killeen: As we get there Danny Kraemer was putting the whole scene together. There were blobs rolled in the cement dust. And we were like, what is this? Danny was putting it together. You've got to understand. When the buildings came down the people that were still inside the buildings were being ground up. It's horrendous to think that, but that's what was going on. They're being taken apart on the way down. The buildings just crumpled. So now that's going through your mind and as you got closer you saw airplane parts. There was a piece of the landing gear, there's a wheel on it. Now you look up into the buildings and you're just looking up and your mind doesn't comprehend what happened. Because you've been there before, the World Trade Center was standing and now it's down to a big, giant smoldering pile of rubble. Other buildings got hit by debris on the way down. It was like an erector set that had come down and pieces pierced buildings next to it. There were thin pieces of structural steel maybe two or three floors high that had speared another building next to it. It was just absolutely bizarre. You've seen collapsed buildings, but nothing like this, never, never. So we're going around and then there were some firemen that I guess knew how to work heavy equipment on their part time job and they were starting to move collapsed fire engines. Fire engines that had parts of the building on them. They're starting to pick them up so they can gain access to the World Trade Center. Now this is all before number Seven fell. We're trying to figure out where to fit into this whole thing. Where we can get in to help? Sometime in there number Seven starts to fall and I'm with John Sigano. I don't recall this, very foggy. I don't know why it's foggy, but he says I grabbed him and pushed him into an alleyway when number Seven was coming down. It just dropped. I don't know if I heard a rumble or what. We just started moving. I grabbed John and pushed him down this alleyway. It's at a right angle to where ever the building was. He told me I did that, then the group of us, we split up. Either like six and six or seven and seven, no matter what number it was. And I went into this hotel. They were stretching I think three inch hose up to the upper floors into the standpipe system to hook into a portable deluge set out the window to put out the fire that started in the Deutsche Bank building. Parts of the plane had fallen into that and that was on fire.

There was an engine there. Everything was so surreal. A friend of mine is in a fireboat museum. The fireboat actually works and I don't know if it was his fireboat or another fireboat. They were pumping a supply line from the Hudson River going into the fire engine and then into the building. So we did get water from the Hudson.

Because New York City's got a different set of fittings, where we would have three inch hose with two and a half inch couplings on it so everything would be backwards compatible, they would have three inch hose with three inch fittings. Stretching into the standpipe, we knew how to do that from working in the projects all the time. That was like a no brainer. But now getting a set of fittings to put it all together, that was something we weren't accustomed to because our fittings were like one two and you're in. And New York City was something different that we're not used to working with. It took a minute to get that figured out.

So we helped them set up the deluge sets there. I remember Scott Richardson was with me. I forget who else was with me. A couple of us, we were stretching stuff up a couple of flights of stairs because no elevators work. There's no power at all there. When the buildings came down, everything went out. I guess when they put the buildings up it was a good idea to run a lot of utilities through there. Who would have thought this was ever going to happen.

So we did that for a while. Then we came downstairs and we're starting to look around. The group kept getting more fractured. It was just ad hoc and it was still daylight out. We start looking to see if we could find anybody on the pile of debris. It never came together in my mind at that time that a hundred ten stories were compacted into the ground. Years later when I would see when they were excavating, it just all fell into a giant tub. I just couldn't imagine at the time. Everything was down in that tub. Even though beforehand I had taken subway rides there. I knew what it was, but my mind couldn't put it together at that time. Now I'm on top of the structure. I recall one guy was there with a dog, a golden retriever and the dog was an actual working dog looking for bodies and stuff. And the dog's name was Bear. I found out that the dog had died. I can't recall how I found out. I talked to somebody that was over there and they knew the dog. They said that the dog died probably from all the ground up cement that they're inhaling.

So we're on top of everything and now a fireman, a New York City fireman comes up to me. I had my white helmet from work. He goes, "Chief, this is just body recovery right now. You've got to understand that." And that's when it hit me that this guy was right. Anybody that's out is out. This is just, as he said, this is just body recovery. I got everything in focus after that. I don't know why he came up to me. You're looking at the massive pieces of steel and construction just lying around, the debris. You try thinking, "Okay, how do we start moving this to get to the people?" It was more than you could put together right at that instant.

To me the unsung heroes were the construction companies that came in and started pulling things apart. That's what you needed. There was nothing else to do. That was pretty much the day. A lot of things were shut down. A lot of power, a lot of transmission devices like for cell phones and stuff. That was shut down. So now I'm trying to think, my family knows I'm supposed to be home. I'm not home. They've got no connection with me. I've got no connection with them. I didn't realize how much I put them in a lurch. They didn't know where I was in relation to the collapse or anything. I'm trying to think how to get hold of my daughter and my wife. My wife was at work. I knew she would be working with the helicopter; she would be on standby as a paramedic. So I'm trying to get hold of my daughter and I couldn't. There was nothing there. So now towards the end of the day, we were looking for something helpful to do. But at the point, after you start stretching a few lines and got things settled down, there was no more to do. So then darkness is coming.

Now we try to get out. For some reason everybody else split up. I don't know how anybody else got back. I made my way down to a dock and there was a boat leaving to go to Liberty State Park, another police boat or Coast Guard boat. I'm not sure. So I walked down to the boat, went across to Liberty State Park. I think somebody else might have been with me. I'm not sure. Got over to Liberty State Park and there are a lot of ambulances that were staged there. Now everybody's getting the idea that, okay, there are no more bodies. No more live bodies coming out. So they started to move. I hitched a ride with one ambulance and they dropped me back off at Five Truck. Then I made contact with my daughter, let her know that I was alive. That was about it.

I went back again one time. I went back with twelve other guys. We met at the Academy one night. The reason I went back is I had a drive in me to do something that was meaningful over there. Not to go there and put up a mark that I was here two times, nothing like that. I just thought maybe there's somebody still alive inside. So we went over there with three pickup trucks full of guys. I guess each one had like a crew cab in it. We get there and now the National Guard is there. I remember it was warm. So I take off my clothes. I'm just in my underwear; put my turnout gear on top of that. And we're walking up toward the National Guard guy. He challenges us and says, "Well do you guys have any ID? Nobody did. He goes, "Well, can you vouch for these guys?" I remember Joe Mahoney was there. So I go, "He's with me. He's with me. He's with me. He's with me. He's with me. He's with me. And I'm with them." And Mahoney is going, "I want to see how you're going to do this because now I'm at the end." Because he knew I was just in my underwear. I had had no idea. So the guy's looking at me like we're all crazy. And he goes, "Go," That's how they went. Go to the site.

So, we went to the site and Billy Weidele was there. We go on top of the pile and we find a hole. We go down into this hole. It's just him and me. In the beginning there are a couple of us and then we start breaking up again. Everybody's going a little bit left and right. So Billy's going down into a hole and he's going down deeper and deeper. We get to a part and I recognize that we're in the elevator room. Because there's just motors for the elevators. And that's when it hit me. People told me everything's buried now. That's when it hit me that we're underground. We're maybe fifteen twenty feet under the top of the pile. I'm looking at the elevator motor and then I say to myself, "Okay now I understand. Everybody's dead." This is the top of the building and it's all down into the hole. That's when my mind just registered the whole thing. We went home that night and that was it. I never went back because I put it together in my head that there was going to be a lot of digging, a lot of time, and that's what it was. I just went over there the two times and that was it.

And a funny thing, maybe a week before this we were at the Port Authority. We're at the airport, Newark Airport. And we're getting ready for a multi-company drill at the airport, Elizabeth and us. I was talking to one of the cops that was in charge of the whole thing, maybe the police captain. I forget his name now, but this is a regular routine thing. I didn't run into the guy for a long time. I thought maybe he had gone over there and he was involved in the collapse because they lost a lot of Port Authority cops too. So one day I ran into him and his story was that they were going, as soon as they could. They got stuck in traffic in the Holland Tunnel when the buildings came down and that saved his life. So I think if we had left Newark earlier than we had and tried to go that way, we would have been like stopped in traffic too. It's just how it would have played out. You don't know, but that's how I think.

Richardson: They couldn't control what was coming in, you know. Everything was still wide open. And they didn't have that perimeter security or anything like that. You just were walking in. If you had turnout gear, they didn't care. Just do what you can and let's get our guys out. Not realizing and knowing that there were no rescues. But you never want to give that hope up, We pull up to a chief. He's standing there amongst this dust and this powder. You could tell he wasn't a field chief. He was a staff chief that was just out there. And we were like, "Chief what do you need?" He turned around with this bewildered look, the hair was disheveled, and he just said, "I don't know." As we're looking on the ground amongst all this just powder, there was no debris. There was just like snow. There was this one lump. It ended up being a torso. It looked just like a cushion from a couch. I was like, "Holy Christ, like that was somebody."

So there was a building under renovation and there was a hotel next to it. The building that was under renovation was on fire. So the chief said what they wanted us to do was go into the hotel and make sure that there was nobody left in the building. We went in. There was no power of course. I had my light so I kind of stayed in the back. We walked up I don't know how many floors, kicked open I don't know how many doors and checked to see what was going on and made sure there was nobody there. We searched. There was nobody in the hotel and then we came out.

Building Seven hadn't collapsed yet and so we were out on the street. We were with other New York City firemen at the time who were all in absolute silence. So when Building Seven came down it was just a horrendous, rumbling noise that you heard. You just saw people were scrambling. They didn't know what it was. We weren't in visual sight of it. We just heard it. We didn't know if it was another plane coming in. So we just ran and scattered.

Then we split up. I forget who I was with in there, but we had done what we had set out to do first. And then we were looking for what else we could do. When Building Seven collapsed, that only made it really real. Then we went to the pile. It was starting to get a little dusk out and I remember we took a break. We met up with everybody else and there were civilians that were coming around. They were bringing water and everything. And so we had water. I remember sitting outside a church, like a store front church and the dust was so thick on everything that you could write on it. Somebody had written some words, God bless the firemen. But I remember sitting outside on the wall and people coming up. They had dust masks on and they had bottles of water for us, giving us bottles of water. I remember a couple of pictures being taken. Then we walked more towards where the pile was. The fire engines that were there, they were just mangled. On some of them the lights were still going.

They grabbed them and dragged them out of way, a couple of them. Some of them were just where they had been parked. We didn't bring tools with us because we didn't have extra tools in the firehouse, so we just went over. I remember going through the compartments. There was nothing left on the rigs. They had taken everything off of them to use. We found a couple of tools and we were able to do some stuff with those, but I remember just coming down there with dust, the dust and the rigs just sitting there in that haze. Just destroyed and just being like wow. And then we came on the pile. There was a cone. It was a cone. We saw a little rubber coat. It was all cleared off, this rubber coat. We didn't realize that we were right outside of a parking garage. We were at street level. We were only on a few maybe feet of the pile in the street. You know, it wasn't the big pile. And this coat that looked like it had been laid out on the pavement was actually a fireman. It was somebody that was probably out in the street. Being that it was a big fire, he was probably somebody from headquarters. Somebody that had turned; his back was to the building. He was face down away from the building. Probably when all of it started to collapse, he started to run toward the parking garage, but never made it. And he was right there. It was like "wow".

Then we worked on the pile through the evening. There was nothing. There were no surface victims. There was no sound. There was nothing. Then we kind of regrouped. It was very disorganized at that point. They hadn't had control over it, so there's nothing here we can really do. I don't even think they had lights and stuff like that for the pile.

The first couple of days of that were pretty messed up, but then after they got a control over it and got rid of all the freelancing, then they had groups like Task Force One. Task Force One was heavy, heavy rescue type stuff with specific groups to tunnel in and do that. Mike Sorace was attached to that

We did run into another group of Newark guys. I think one or two guys that had gotten over there that kind of joined in. I guess we ended up being about fourteen guys at the end. But that was about it. A lot of Newark guys spent a lot of days there. What we thought was probably being helpful, probably wasn't being helpful. A couple of chiefs that we talked to had no clue on what should be done, who should do it, and who they were even reporting to.

So we left. I guess it was around midnight. We got a boat that could take us back over to Liberty State Park. When we got back over there, it was just ambulances lined up as far as you could see. There was a whole task force type thing that they put in. My uncle lives in West Milford. I had his cell phone number and I called him. I says, "Where are you?" "I'm at Liberty State Park." I'm like, "wow." It turned out he was further back because he came in from West Milford. There was one group of ambulances that was going to transport us back to the firehouse. So I couldn't go down and see my uncle because my ride was leaving. I said, "Wow, West Milford is down here." A lot of the guys went back the next day.

Pierson: They were pulling a couple of guys out of a rig that was partially buried and the look on their face, you know. It was pretty surreal; there were parts of plane right where we were standing. That was weird, really weird.

We helped dig out lines for the first couple of hours and tried to help them get some water supply established. They had a front loader. They were clearing the streets. The guy was a pro. I mean he opened up the street. It wasn't totally clean, but it was a nice job of getting things cleared. That was some of the logistics, some of the stuff you had to do.

Then they let us get up on the pile and we started searching. It got to be seven or eight o'clock at night and a Battalion Chief went up to the top to the highest point I guess you could. He said, "I want everybody's attention. We haven't set up adequate lighting here. I don't think it's that safe, but if one of you guys can give me a good reason to keep going, I'm not going to pull the plug out." And nobody spoke. I mean, you kind of knew it really was recovery. It really wasn't a rescue operation at that point. Everybody knew.

We came home. I don't remember how the hell we got home. I know we didn't take the boat back. I have no idea how we got home. I couldn't tell you. We went back a couple of days. I went back in my pickup truck with the guys from the firehouse. I did drive and drive back. That's it. You were doing the same thing day after day.

Alexander: Well, when I got there the first thing we saw was the mangled buildings and still that cloud, that dust that was still in the air. Seeing firefighters just sitting there, just totally worn out, covered in the building dust. It was devastating. It looked like a war zone. Or even like Godzilla had walked through there. It's hard to describe. It just set in your mind and it made me realize, "Hey what's going on here? Is the world coming to an end here?" Because I had never experienced anything like it. That just made me put my job into perspective. What I do? All you heard were the PASS alarms, the constant beeping and then having to like go through the rubble searching for people.

Highsmith: First thing you notice is it looked like snow all across the ground, but it was concrete dust. You looked at the New York firefighters. They got that blank stare, looking at the ground, won't look you in your eyes, with no command structure in place. We were ready and available to work, but we really didn't go to work that day. We came home that night. But after that, I worked the bucket brigade for about a week or two. The last night I was there with Anthony Tambori, Mike Gibbons, Jimmy Pierson, and Phil Spagnola. We were in full gear. As we were coming out, because I was a black guy with four white guys, the news cameras, everybody wanted to interview. So I said, "This is the brotherhood we have. No problem here."

They offered us four course meals then police cars came to pick us up, take us to some bar, everybody treated us well. We go to the next bar. Before I knew it, it was four o'clock in the morning. We got no money. We're in full gear. We have no idea what part of New York we're in. So we just walked into a bar, explained our situation, drank some more while they sent us a limousine. The limousine took us home.

I thought the country was the best it's ever been at that moment. I was hoping it would stay that way, but it didn't. It went back to normal, right.

Petrone: At that time it was early and so it still was all bucket brigades, passing buckets down still looking for body parts. Personally I didn't recover anything. It was the twelfth, thirteenth, fourteenth, fifteenth, whatever. It was right after the Trade Center. It may have been a day later, but it was more or less just long lines of people with buckets at the top filling them and passing them down. People at the bottom sifting through, looking for bone fragments and anything that can identify anybody. It was tough to stay there. The smell was no good.

Straile: We got there. I heard the PASS alarms, but hey, you had to do what you had to do. They didn't know if there were still people alive at the time. It wasn't a recovery effort then. It was still a rescue effort, it wasn't recovery yet.

Basically we were on the pile doing things. One day they asked us to go up to some roof tops and check. We went up on the roof once or twice. Most of it was going through the pile and digging through.

We came back a couple of days by bus. One day we're getting ready to leave. The chief in charge of our crew, he said, "Look we're getting ready to go guys. Thanks a lot." They wouldn't allow the buses back in the area where they dropped us off to get us. So we said, "How the hell are we going to get out of here?" They shut down an area and we couldn't get out. So somebody said, "Well look, they're bringing people over on the boat across the river from Jersey City. So we went down to one of the boats, talked to the captain. Are you going back to Jersey City? Yeah. So we got on the boat and there were like eight or ten of us got on this boat. He took us back to Exchange Place in Jersey City. They dropped us off on the dock.

Now where do we go? What do we do? Everybody's filthy in their turnout clothes, boots, and helmets. So what do we do now? "Well, I guess we could take the train. It's running." "The train?" "Yeah, the PATH train." So now we're all down there. Nobody has money. There are a couple of Port Authority cops standing there. "Where are you guys heading?" "We're going back to Newark." "The train should be coming in any minute." "Oh, okay but we ain't got no cash." "We'll open the gate for you." And there's eight or ten guys going through the gate. Filthy, dirty, covered with soot from the World Trade Center and go through. The train pulls up and it was loaded. It had a lot of people. I said, "We can't get on." The cop says, "Get on. They'll move." Gets on, "Everyone get out of the way. Let these firemen on." So we got on. With that, everyone that was sitting down got up and started to clap. You guys are great. Took us back to Newark. Special Service, we called them. They came. One of the guys had his cell phone, he called them. Came up with two vans, picked us up and took us back to Twenty Engine. True story for the World Trade Center. I'll never forget that because of the people, what they did on the train. Here are these people in suits, ties, all clean. And ten filthy firemen, they got up. Thank you. You know, it was good.

A couple of days later when they said it became recovery that's when we stopped going back. There was no sense to going back.

Freese: What I remember was almost total chaos and devastation. I felt like I was back somewhere in World War I. We just lost a sense of everything. There was nothing we could do. We got no directions from police officers or firefighters that were there and had suffered a huge loss. It just had happened so there was no organization of any type. But the one thing that got to me, the reason I never went back is because I could hear the PASS alarms. For those who don't know, PASS alarm is a protective device you wear. If you stay motionless more than forty-five seconds it beeps a high piercing sound so it notifies your fellow firefighters that somebody is either motionless, down, unconscious or something. I heard it everywhere and I knew that each one of those PASS alarms was a fellow firefighter and I couldn't do anything about it. All the guys outside with their hands on their heads. There was no one to lead. I came back home and I never went back.

Dainty: One of the weird things was the amount of dust and papers that were floating around. It was just unreal. The smoke was like, if you've ever been to a dump fire, that was the odor that you kept getting. It was from the combination of building materials, asbestos, paper; it was like being at a dump that was burning.

Griffith: We pulled up and just as we pulled up, Seven came down. We were getting off, we were on the dock and the dust came through. We hadn't done a thing yet. We're all gagging and coughing loaded with this dust. I remember going up and there was a fireman there working a pump. He was covered in dust and he was pumping. He was in shorts. And he was just a mess. They were hooking up a line, so we went right away to give him a hand. We kind of organized that. He was saying this is crazy. He had been there the whole time. So Norman kind of said, "I'm going to do some recon and find out where we're going." They told us that there was a staging area up by the high school up by West Street. So we made our way. We had actually climbed through the winter guard off an escalator that wasn't working, crawled all the way up to get on the street to go. So we would have been on the north side of everything. But climbing through them it was just crazy to see this insanity.

We got up there and we got to the staging area. We were there a while. We're saying, "We're here. We're all broken down." They're going thank you. Then you're sitting there and you realize, they're not going to put you to work. They're not putting you in harm's way. The word kind of got out to all the groups that were there. So basically what you did is you got up as your group and you kind of sauntered back down. We're obviously violating protocol and all nine yards.

You got down there and you just tried to help, whatever you could do. You know, you jump in. I remember a group of guys getting over in one area and they started to help and some New York firemen said, "Hey, get the "F" out of here. And we're whoa, whoa, what's up? You know and we kind of sauntered over and asked, "Wait a minute these guys are here to help. Why are you yelling at them?" They go, "This is where our chief is. We're getting our chief out." So there was a lot of that.

I mean the buildings were a hundred and ten stories. Basically the pile was maybe three stories. Where'd it go? You think about that grey dust, everything concrete, but think about it, each floor about an acre. All sheetrock, that's what that grey dust was, all that sheetrock, two acres per floor.

I remember an SUV going by. It had railings, these guys in these black outfits, machine guns, hanging off the rails on the side. And you're saying what? But the vehicle going by was like a car going through snow. You know, when you get a good snow fall, a car goes through, the muffled sound? That's what this was, but this was just dust. There was no snow. It was just dust. It was just crazy. You had a guy walking through with a spray bottle with water in it and a rag. And he goes, "You need an eye wash. You really need this. I'm a nurse and you're doing damage to your eyes." He was spraying people's faces and wiping them down. There were people coming up to you with sandwiches from the restaurants. So out of all this chaos, you're seeing so much humanity at the same time through all this craziness.

You wonder who was organizing things because at that time they started to move vehicles, They started getting dumpsters in there with little Bobcats to pick up the dust and the debris so they could get in close to start working. This was like, you're talking five o'clock or later. I was amazed that even though it was so crazy, things that were kicking in.

We stayed through the night and helped and did whatever we could. The sun was coming up and there was a boat going back. I said, "I'm going to go back." I really didn't think that they were going to find anybody else. Actually a couple of hours later they did, those people that were stuck in that one stairwell and that was probably at one o'clock in the afternoon. But I just looked at it and said there's no way they're finding anybody alive here.

Roberson: We went over to help so they gave you all this stuff, your mask, your googles, hard hat. It was a sight to see. It was a sight to see.

West: We had probably one of the Newark commanders, maybe Chief Esparolini, I believe was in charge of us. Told us all to sit tight until he can find out what we could do. And I think as it turned out, we sat there for a while. Some guys broke off and tried to go help, but as it turned out the first night on September eleventh, I don't think anybody knew really what to do. Everything had just fallen. There were buildings that were still in danger of falling. It was an eerie feeling because no one seemed really to know what to do at that point. We sort of hung around for a few hours and then we actually got back on the boat and came back unfortunately. Because at that point I don't think there was anybody organizing the pile, you know the infamous pile where you were digging, looking for people. I don't think at that point that had even started yet. It was so new. It was the same day. But we honestly didn't do much on the first day. Most of us went back days after, you know, however many days people went and that's when you actually were digging on the pile and doing different things. But the first night, not much was going on.

Willis: I went up to a young kid that was sitting on a fire engine. He had his head down. He was a probationary. Felt sorry for him because I was fairly new myself on the job. I asked him, "Is there anything I can do to help?" And he turned around and said, "There's nothing you can do. I lost my whole battalion." The only one he knew of that was alive was him and his chief. So a bunch of guys were grabbing stuff and helping. Me and Billy Melodic wind up going off on our own making our way around ground zero. We don't have to talk about what we've seen. I'd rather not speak about what was seen.

We went in and tried our best to help. At one point we were so confused. It looked like Arnold Schwarzenegger in the beginning of The Terminator. It felt like a movie. It didn't feel real. Everything felt fake. I can't explain it any other way. It was like being in the movie. It didn't look real to me. Me and Billy walked through the Bank of America I think it was. The bank was wide open, one of the biggest banks in the world wide open. We walked right through. Everything was wide open, I mean, it was unbelievable to see the devastation. When we walked out of the bank, the whole street was nothing but cars on fire. How? We're trying to figure out how? You know with the buildings coming down. There really was no fire other than

Building Seven I believe it was at that time. Guys were fighting that. And that was pretty much the base of it.

Then they brought us to the atrium that night. They washed our eyes out and then nurses worked on us, me and Billy. They cleaned our eyes out, our noses. We didn't have breathing apparatus available. We brought our tanks with us, but hid them because we ran out of air in twenty minutes and there were no re-fills. So when we went back we were filthy dirty. They cleaned our ears out, our noses, they actually had women there that gave us new clothes and then nurses were massaging. All the men were in cots. They laid us in cots in the atrium and they gave us massages. They let us lay down because we were there a long time.

Then when we woke up, we walked out and they had a gigantic truck with all telephones. Verizon put that out. We were able to contact our families to let them know we were okay. I called my wife, my family, made sure, they knew we were okay. Don't worry about it. They were panicking. I mean, as much as we went through, I think they went through worse. My children were confused because they were maybe ten and twelve at the time. They're taken out of school. It was a rough time, the kids were scared. I don't talk about work at home, so they were really confused. And my wife was worried. My mother-in-law was devastated until she saw my face, then she was happy. It was three days that we were there. It was rough. You know things that you saw guys go through. And it wasn't as rough on us as much as seeing the faces of the men who lost their guys; that was hard. When they carried Father Judge off, you could see everybody took that really bad.

We went back for three days. They had a boat right at the atrium. There was a marina. They would pick you up there and they were going back and forth, shuttling, giving breaks to everyone. Everyone would go home, see their family, clean up, wash up. You'd get back together. Everybody was going back and forth. I think a lot of guys went, even some retired guys went. I can't remember. It was an interesting experience. I'll never want to experience anything like that again. I don't think anybody will experience that again unless we go to war.

Centanni: You heard the PASS alarms. You hear engines growling. But with that I don't even know if this makes sense; there was an eerie silence. The things you think you would have heard you didn't hear. Talking, commotion, hustle and bustle, you didn't hear any of that. I'll never forget walking off the pier, getting all our people ready to go toward Church Street and a New York company of guys must have been walking back, didn't even look at you. Not in a mean way, they were just white from head to toe with dust and carrying their tools with their heads down and just walked over. I remember them just sitting against the building as we're walking by. They walked by us. We walked by them. I think there might have been a couple of just like, "What's up? What's up?" It was crazy.

We walk out. We're looking. We don't know what to do, so Norman said, "I want all the companies to stay here." He took me and another captain with him to look for the command post and what's going on. We find a group of bosses. I remember this clearly, that Norman's like, "I got like thirty guys here. We're broken up. We got some tools with us. What could we do?" And the one chief says to him, "Boss, I appreciate you coming. The best thing you could do for us is go up to Church Street. They're staging people or go home and come back tomorrow because I just got called in. We don't even know who's running our department." So Norman goes, "Well, where's the command post? Who's in charge?" He goes, "Right now, I think I'm in charge. The command post is over there." They point at a pile of rubble with cones on it and a bunch of guys standing around it. He goes, "They're all dead. They're all buried over there." That was the most sobering experience. Norman's looking at me. I'm looking at him. He's like, "I don't know what we do here." So we go back to our guys. We're going to march up to Church Street. So we go through the rubble. We had to go through one of the smaller buildings, those little bridges that you go through. We went through that rubble. We get back up there. So basically that night we didn't do anything. This is around seven o'clock September Eleventh. We stay until about midnight. We didn't really do much of anything. Walked around, talked to a few people. Help out a few fireman, you know, cleaning them up.

I always described it as a Godzilla movie experience. It looked like the movie we watched about Godzilla, the firetrucks were smashed like toys, buildings upside down, everything turned over. And I have to say this. I didn't see one body. I didn't see a body.

None of us. We didn't see a body during that, just total destruction. Concrete, firetrucks, ambulances, and cars, everything was smashed.

So that was our experience that night. I wound up going back subsequently. We dug on the pile. Giuliani and our government allowed you to believe that you were doing some kind of rescue operation which was probably a brilliant move, but then they knew it was over. There was nobody getting rescued. I think they let that process happen. They let the guys work to keep the hope going. But that was my experience. That night we were there. We didn't accomplish much.

But the guys that were all willing to go, brave, lined up, ready to go. Just let us get out there to help. What could we do? Other Newark guys like Gibbins and a few guys went that day. They watched building Seven come down as they got there. They were just going, "You got to get out here with people. This is crazy."

So we spent a few trips. I didn't make as many as some guys who were there every day. I was there maybe two more times after that. That was the 9/11 experience. For me it was vivid. It was clear. I'll never forget that night driving over. It was a crazy moment.

Gail: When we got there it was chaos. There was nothing to do because there was no structure. There was no direction, as you would expect in something of that magnitude. Not putting down anybody, but that's kind of what we expected when we got there. So it was very difficult to even really get anything done because it was so confusing. You didn't know where to go. What was safe? What was not safe?

What needed to be done? We didn't have any equipment. All we had was the gear on our back. Most of the stuff there was destroyed. The hierarchy was already killed, many of them. There was no communications. We didn't have radios. We couldn't communicate with New York City. I don't even think New York City knew we were there. Probably forty-five, fifty people came that night. Looking back at it, it wasn't that productive, us being there. Nobody was recovered anyway. So none of it was productive, but even our efforts weren't that productive because of the lack of direction, communications, and incident command structure, the whole thing. It was hard to get anything relevant done.

I went back a couple more days. We started driving in. I don't know how many days after I went back. It was within the week, but it may have been three or four days. I think you needed to show ID. I don't think they were letting too many people in or out. So we went in. The Port Authority was checking. It was almost like check points at the bridges and tunnels. You had to show ID, where you were going, and stuff like that then they would let us in. We went down to lower Manhattan and just parked anywhere. By that time there was definitely more structure. They definitely had a lot. It was pretty quick, actually, how they organized considering the loss. And there was definitely a little more direction on what needed to be done, how to get it done.

We went with our own crew so we had internal control. All Newark people were working pretty much with Newark people because we went with a pretty big group of people, pretty good numbers. Then we split up as we needed to and then we would just get involved with whoever was working. There was no "We need you here. We need you there." It was like, "Hey, go to work." You would go on the pile and start removing rubble by hand and in buckets and start passing them out. That's pretty much what we did.

West: We had one the Newark commanders, Chief Esparolini, I believe was in charge of us. Told us all to sit tight until he can find out what we could do. I think as it turned out, we sat there for a while. Some guys broke off and tried to go help, but as it turned out the first night on September eleventh, I don't think anybody knew really what to do. Everything had just fallen. There were buildings that were still in danger of falling. It was an eerie feeling because no one seemed really to know what to do at that point. So we sort of hung around for a few hours and then we actually got back on the boat and came back unfortunately. Because at that point I don't think there was anybody organizing the pile, the infamous pile where you were digging, looking for people. I don't think at that point that had even started yet. It was so new. It was the same day. But we honestly didn't do much on the first day. Most of us went back days after, however many days people went and that's when you actually were digging on the pile and doing different things. But the first night, not much was going on.

Early on you weren't allowed to drive through the tunnels. So you had to show your badge. We drove our own cars and piled a bunch of guys into them. We made our way over there. I probably was over there five or six times early on. If I remember correctly, you just flashed your badge and they were allowing you to come through. But otherwise they weren't allowing regular traffic. So you went there as much as you could and tried to help or do whatever you could to make a difference. But at some point I think they all realized that there wasn't any more saving going on. It was just a recovery process. I think they found that out pretty early. So you went over there and did what you could. Being a firefighter, you did what you could do to help.

Prachar: We didn't do much of anything that first night. I went back a couple of days later. We took a couple of buses over and this time we didn't make the same mistake of the first night. All these guys from all these towns are standing there outside the yellow tape barricades and the Newark guys did what we do best. We did an end run around, through a building, out of the building. There we are at Ground Zero. Went through a building, out of a building and went to work.

Digging, passing buckets, at one point we were on a pile, digging down, and trying to get down lower. This one New York Chief comes over, starts screaming and yelling at us all because we were actually right underneath a section of the Twin Towers that hadn't fallen. It was probably four, five stories tall. If this thing would have given way, we were dead. So we got chased off the pile and went somewhere else, started digging there. Went somewhere else started passing the buckets.

Me, Don Gilmartin, and George Jorda ended up on the roof of a hotel and found plane wreckage and body parts. So we tried to get somebody from EMS in to bring some body bags up. They did. We had a couple of construction workers with us and one young Spanish guy. He was devastated. That smell was just there, decaying flesh. As soon as we hit the one roof of this one hotel, that's all you could smell. We found a leg, a woman's leg. You knew it was a woman's leg because the toe nails were painted, a perfectly intact leg. I just thought this kid was going to lose it. I said to him, "Pal, you don't have to do this. You're a carpenter. You're not trained to deal with this stuff. Don't kill yourself." He says, "No. These people are Americans. I'm not leaving." I never caught his name. I'll probably never see the guy again in my life, but he just impressed the hell out of me. He was willing to stick it out because it was the right thing to do.

George and I are making our way to where Engine Ten and Truck Ten are which is right at the backend of the twin towers. We start heading over there. They're chasing everybody out because there's something going on. They're moving some stuff. People need to leave the area so we start making our way back west and we pass by a hotel. In the first floor of the hotel is a bar and all the windows are blown out. But there are a couple of construction workers in there like taking a break sitting there. So what do George and I do? We go inside.

Well, the guy's pouring booze. He's got booze. But he's got no compressed air. He's got the CO_2 for beer from the tap, but he has no flashlight and no way to see what he's doing downstairs. I've got my little Survivor light with me. He says, "Can you give me a hand? First one's on me." Like the guy's really charging. So, what do I do? I bring this guy downstairs. We make our way into the area where the kegs are. I help him tap a couple of barrels. We go back upstairs and here I am, I'm standing there is what's left of lower Manhattan. Me and George having a beer; toasting our departed brothers. That was the day George Bush came. And we were heading back to the buses because the buses were leaving at a certain time. And I was supposed to go to Pat's niece's rehearsal dinner. She was getting married the next day. I said, "You know what? I'm blowing this rehearsal dinner off. I'm going back. I'll find my way back home somehow." As we're starting to head back, a couple of guys were coming back and they said that Bush was going to be there in a few minutes, everything was cordoned off. You weren't getting in. Not the way we did the first time. There was nothing to do. So I got back on the bus and we left.

Nasta: Chief Esparolini found somebody in the command post somewhere in New York City. We just went on there and we started working as a bucket brigade, if you remember those long lines with the plastic buckets. We started that and we kept going up and up. We worked there through the night until probably about maybe seven o'clock the next morning. And at seven o'clock the next morning we were told, go back home. They put us back on the Coast Guard cutter, back to Bayonne.

I continued to go there because everybody was kind of doing their own thing at that point. It didn't seem to my eyes that the

Newark Fire Department did anything organized to go over there and help with this effort. We kept meeting in different spots. I went there for an entire week, the entire first week. We were always going over at night. We started at night. They had made the work shifts from six at night to six in the morning, so I kept going over at night. I think that last day I went there, I went during the day which was probably the following Saturday. I think after that they said, "Listen guys, this is recovery, you know, we're battening the hatches down." All the USAR teams from all over the country had come in. All that loose help which was pretty much us doing our thing, kind of went away. And that was it. The last day I didn't go over with our guys. I went over with the Hackensack Fire Department. They had a bus going over. And we went over by bus. On the way back they had the bus pick us up at the Waterways taxi, you know the ferries that go back and forth. We went back on a ferry.

There's no record of me being there because we're fire department. We're supposed to be there. I never took any pictures while I was there. Turns out guys have pictures of themselves, but I never took a picture. The only picture and I don't know where it is, but when we were on the way back that day, a woman on the ferry asked, "Would you be kind enough to take a picture with my son?" Little guy, little seven maybe eight year old boy, and that was the only picture that was taken. It was on that ferry and I've never seen the picture. I know I was in it because the woman took it. Don't know who the woman was, but I have no record whatsoever of me ever being there. I tried to sign up for that cancer fund that they have for the responders that went there. And the funny story is, I opened up the website and I keep putting my name in. Now my name is Michael Nasta and I just turned sixty. They would ask me my age. And every time I put my name in and my age, a New York City fireman from Brooklyn that's named Michael Nasta comes up and it tells me I'm already registered. And to this day I cannot register in that website. I don't know, God forbid, if something happens, I can't register. Every time I put my name in that guy comes up. We were there. We did some digging. We recovered some people and obviously like everybody else, saw some horrible sights.

Rodrigues: Once I got there it was like watching a movie. I still remember. It was like watching a movie, one of those war movies that you see that everything is like destroyed. It's just crazy. Actually we walked through Church Street. I remember the color of all that dust and debris. We stayed there until probably two o'clock in the morning. They put us back on the boat. The Coast Guard brought us back here to Newark. Went back to work my second day. At eighteen hundred hours back to the World Trade Center. And I was there for I would say the first three days. The next morning I stayed there. They provided all the firemen with clothing, water, and so on. The third day, that's when I saw the reality. There were a lot of body parts, EMS carrying bodies, dead bodies out of the area. We worked at the pile where we discovered a lot of people that were dead. There were people that had survived. I guess it was not their turn to go.

Ramos: When we get there it's chaos. They weren't organized yet. They were still waiting on the proper personnel to come in. What they needed. And Esparolini went and spoke to them, spoke to their commander. They told us to sit down and wait for a while. So as we're waiting, you see this crane, big crane comes out with at least a hundred, a hundred and fifty, two hundred men hanging on it, iron workers, going through here. They're trying to get to the site. Without the iron workers it wouldn't have been done. We didn't get to work that night because I guess they weren't ready and they didn't want to put us in danger. Some guys did stay, but I didn't work that night. I know somehow I got back. I didn't stay there. I forget how I got back from New York. That's something. I don't know how we rolled back. It was in a boat? I don't recall. I don't recall. I guess the shock I don't recall at all how I got back. I remember it was late. I know we stayed. It had to be three or four in the morning by the time we got back. We waited that long.

So the next day I went with Taz, Deblin , though the tunnel because they were only accepting emergency personnel at that time going through there. We got through. We checked in with some chief from the New York fire department and he gave me a working area. So we go to the pile and the pile, you can't describe it. Ten stories tall, not a sign of a desk, not a sign of any type of office equipment, nothing that you would think would be office equipment, just a pile of concrete, iron, and wire. That's all you saw, concrete. You didn't see a telephone; you didn't see a typewriter; you didn't see a chair. I guess that was all pulverized coming down. You didn't see anything like that. You smelled death.

I went on two occasions, that night and the second day. I went there first, came back late so I didn't go back. It was the second full day of the incident that I went back. So it was hot. That why you smelled the death. You wouldn't smell it on the ground. You actually smelled it in the buckets, the buckets themselves. I guess they were saturated with the blood of all those that passed. One by one, the buckets would come by. You would smell bodies starting to rot. Then you would walk up to an area, you could smell someone there. Besides that were the PASS alarms going off. You could hear them close to you, you could hear them far away. You could hear them all over the place.

I was in a spot where there was an I-beam over me. I'm taking it out rock by rock and a New York chief comes over to me. He goes, "Hey Newark." He saw I'm from Newark. He goes, "Hey buddy, I know there's someone there, but I'm telling you you're in bad spot. Could you please come out of there?" I look at the beam over me. He goes, "I'd prefer you not be there." I said, "Alright, but we know there's someone there. I smell them too, basically."

I only went once myself. I never went back after that because the job was immense. It looked as though it was going to take years, not, like they were saying, months. It looked like it would take years to go through all of that. It was amazing. It was like living in a valley of mountains. There were structures that were ten stories high. There was a drop. Then you had to come back out to where they were rigging a rope across to slide who they found, the parts they found. There was never a whole body found. Through a system of ropes, that's the way they were passing them down. It was amazing. I got the smell, then the desperation. You say, "There's no one alive. There's no one alive there."

It was basically a recovery operation. But I'll tell you what, there was a big difference from the first night I went there to that second day. Because now they had all kinds of things out there. Now all the people were in place, emergency police, FBI, Red Cross. If you needed Chap Stick, they had Chap Stick. They were giving out boots, if you needed boots. I don't know why they had boots out there, but there were boots, jeans, toothpaste, anything you needed. What the rescuers need, they had there. So that second day was a tremendous, tremendous difference. You could see how they got together. They started getting stricter as well, as far as letting people in. Because some guys were freelancing going to certain areas and doing it themselves. Then they got tighter and tighter on that aspect of it. There was only one way to walk in and you have to go to certain people and sign up at a certain time, be there only a certain time. You shouldn't be there that long. So once it got to that point, I said no going back, because at that point they also only wanted New York guys in there which I understand. That's their job. Those are their guys. They want to go get them. So I only went that first night and the second day. Went twice. It was something you'll never forget.

DeCeuster: So the next morning I went over with Steve Ciasullo. We drove through the Holland Tunnel. Not a car in the tunnel. I'm like, "Ho, stop here we got to take a picture." We had all our gear in the truck. Cops were good about that. We were there for three days, until they really didn't let you go back anymore.

When we got there we were trying to get in working, doing stuff. I think it was the second day. A lot of Newark guys went over there. They went over that first night. I think they stole a Coast Guard boat. We were out there working. I worked at the pit, right next to the pile was the pit and it was amazing. It was amazing seeing people working together. You know when something came up "shhhhh", thousands of people were silent. We did remove a couple of remains. One was a woman. I guess she was a woman. You couldn't really tell the gender.

George Perdon crawled in a hole to search. So he's crawling in, next thing you know, "shhhhh, quiet, quiet." George comes out of this hole, gray. The whole place went crazy. We have a survivor, a survivor. He was so embarrassed. We went back to where we were hanging out, getting a breather, drinking water, and the Cardinal from New York comes over. "Where's that man? Where's that survivor?" And everyone's pointing at George. "There he is." He was pissed.

That was an amazing. You know what? I wouldn't want to miss it for the world. You knew things were different when there weren't a lot of people at the hospital. The workmanship, the construction workers, everything that worked there was an amazing, for an unfortunate situation it was just totally amazing to me.

Daly: Seeing New York firemen at the time walking by us, they were like zombies, no expressions, no nothing. I wound up being like that, no expression, no nothing.

I got on a rig. Me and Billy Melodic watched the rig with one guy while the other guys got something to eat and got something to drink. None of them wanted to go, but I kind of like forced them. I said, "Guys you got to. Go, go." The one guy that was there with me said, "Thanks a lot. I appreciate it." I said, "No need, you're a brother." It was weird. It was like never never land. I was in the twilight zone. Billy even said the same thing to me because it's that weird. Where were we just now? And it took me about two or three minutes to get over that.

The second time I went over I got a little better because the initial one was the first night and I was like wow. This is not real. I wanted to meet up with Chief Killeen, but I couldn't find him. I was trying to find him. I was trying to get to him. I knew he would be working. Billy and I went off on our own.

Arce: When we got off, it was maybe a foot of soot we were walking in. We couldn't see each other. It was a heavy dust and there were a lot of hot spots, fires all over the place, but we couldn't do anything because we couldn't see. We waited there a couple hours and we came back that same night. The next day I was working and they sent me out on a signal eight. It was Engine Seven and Truck Eleven with two chiefs, McGovern and Snyder. I was the captain on Engine Seven.

We went out to Staten Island. They put us in Staten Island for maybe a good hour and then they told us to go to Ground Zero. We didn't do any water. We parked the rig and we did all searches. We spent the whole day there. Looking for bodies and searching the buildings. I found the duct system in the World Trade Center where I literally went inside it and maybe sixty, seventy-five, a hundred feet going down. I found a flood, but I didn't get to see any bodies or anything. It was a mess.

I spent the whole week there. I came back the next day and spent the whole week. I helped out with the bucket brigades, digging, and looking. But that was an experience you may never forget.

I saw the towers. When we got there, there were about five stories left, but the only thing you could see was a steel beam and there was like a shell. I'm like, "Oh, my God." It's incredible here, incredible, incredible. It just caved, the whole thing disappeared. All the buildings around it were just done. It was just the saddest day.

Johnson: When we got over there it was like complete chaos. The people were walking around like zombies. The soot and dust in the air was insane. They were like a complete nightmare. It was insane just to see. We were walking. When we got to Pace University Captain Volkert's daughter was just petrified and stunned. We took her out; we brought her back. It was just so much that was going on that day. I stayed there for that night and I came back like three other times.

I actually came over there with Mike Sorace because he was part of that USAR team and I think Ray Hatton is part of that team as well. So we went over to see. It was just a massive, massive effort. We went to the Jacob Javits Convention Center where there was a command post. Everything was set up in there. It was kind of eerie to go through the Holland Tunnel and no one was there. You ride down the street you ride up to the Jacob Javits and everybody's clapping and they're like wow because they were thanking you for your services. It was a surreal moment.

So I worked over there. We paired with companies and were working with them. There really was enough to do. You had forty story buildings you could still see were burning besides the other ones. You're looking up. You see the Marriot, everything's blown out, debris everywhere. You see all these helmets, you know, the guys' helmets on the side.

Tarantino: So we kind of split up into a couple of groups. Only because some guys honestly didn't want to go on the pile. What was crazy about it is I think we were lucky enough to where the streets were kind of cleared by the time we got there, the two main arteries. You could still see the big heavy construction trucks. They were picking up cars with the claw and moving them still. But we had access. We could actually walk on the street. So we made that turn to Ten Engine, a bunch of guys. We said we'll all meet back here. I was with Charlie Krutulis, Chief Smith, Jimmy Smith was with me. Esparolini actually ended up coming up a little bit later. But it really was pretty much me and Charlie Krutulis. Charlie's an iron worker. He knows. There was nothing. There was nothing. There was dust and rebar. It was just insane. So we got up on the pile.

There was a lot of smoke. I mean there were a bunch of engine companies, more on the Trade Center Two side. They pretty much put out where we were. So you could get up literally on top of the pile, probably twenty-five, thirty feet high. You're climbing up it and you're literally using the rebar. But the problem was, it was hot. I mean it was crazy hot. So I ended up taking off my coat and I got ripped up. Everybody got ripped up. Because that rebar, it was just everywhere. We ended up getting up on the top of this pile and you could see there were groups of guys definitely together. A lot of New York City guys, a lot of construction guys were there. But Charlie and I kind of worked together and it ended up Chief Smith kind of worked with us also.

So we end up on a pile that is literally, if you're looking down onto where Ten Engine would be, Ten Engine was off to my left. So I could always kind of keep an eye on where Ten Engine was from where we were up on this pile. We made it down to the back side of a pile and we ended up finding this little void space. I was able to kind of slip through it. Charlie wasn't, bigger guy. I was able to slip through it and once I got through it, I tell you it went down about twenty-five feet, maybe thirty feet. It was deep. So Charlie and I worked for about half an hour to just open this up enough. Once we opened it up then the word was we found a new area. We started to go down. They called for the dogs and the microphone. So they brought the dogs and the dogs couldn't smell anything, but it was deep. The dogs couldn't go in where we were. The first time I came up we were waiting for the dogs and then I went back down. Now everybody kind of knows that we found this little spot. There's a bunch of people that are standing around it. As I go back down, one of our chiefs is going, "No, you can't go in there. This and that." and I'm like, "Chief, you're not the chief here. We're going in."

So me and Charlie go down with the sound guy. It probably took us like at least half an hour to get this guy down there. It was sturdy enough. It wasn't like you're watching in the movies where things were falling on you. You could make it in there. I want to say it was probably a four by four hole. You could make your way down there. It kind of curved off and it wasn't straight. It wasn't like you could look down and see through it with a flashlight, but you could kind of wrap your way around it. When we got the sound guy down there and this is the only story I really ever tell my family when they ask about it. You know when those sound guys come they need quiet. The sound guy told me that they can hear a fingernail scratch two hundred feet away, a fingernail scratch, if it's quiet enough. So in the middle of this chaos craziness they would call for complete silence. It's the one thing that still sticks with me today. You know how sometimes silence is loud? Like it's painful? I can remember thinking I'm in the middle of New York City, the busiest city in the world and you can't hear a thing. It was remarkable.

We never found anybody. Never even came close. I never saw any blood. I only saw paper, concrete, crumbled sheet rock, a ton for rebar. I found a rubber goulash, that is the only thing I found and maybe a little shard of carpet. That was it. There was nothing else. When I talk about Chief Smith, I'll tell you, Chief Smith is bad ass. He never brought his Deputy Chief helmet. He brought a fireman helmet. Didn't want to be noticed as a deputy chief. That guy's the man. He worked his ass off. He didn't take a break, nothing.

One other thing I remember. We probably stayed there for about twelve hours, give or take. Maybe a little more, a little less, I can't remember exactly what it was. But they would pull you off of the pile every once in a while. They had these safety teams. Now Deutsche Bank was right next door. There was a slit right in Deutsche Bank. It was crazy. And every time that thing swayed, they would try to pull people off the pile. So, it took us, that whole operation that I told you about, going in the hole. That was probably six, seven hours of pulling stuff out, making it open wide enough, getting people in there, the whole thing. And we weren't just focused on one hole. You start to focus on other things too.

So maybe it's about the third time they're about to pull us off the pile. Jimmy Smith is there and he goes, "I'm not going." It was a pain in the ass. You just climbed up this fucking thing and it'd take you like ten minutes to get down. You have to climb back up and everybody's got to go down and then everybody's got to go back up. After about the third time Jimmy Smith says, "I'm not leaving this pile." So we would go in the hole. We would hide and wait for all clear. We did it probably ten times, probably ten times. He's bad ass. He really is bad ass, that's for sure.

Ten Engine across the street was set up like this triage place. We're eighteen hours after the whole thing happened. They had brought a lot of stuff, a lot of stuff, food and gloves. I couldn't believe how much stuff they had there. They had generators. I mean it was crazy how much stuff they had there. It started to rain a little bit. We went into Ten, got some food, and I felt it was hopeless. You're there for twelve hours and you don't see anything, nothing. There was nothing. But as we started to talk about it, you just knew there was nobody left. I mean there was nothing, really there was nothing. So we left and I never went back. You know, our guys went back a million times. I knew we weren't finding anybody. My only purpose was to go there to find somebody. Hoping we could find somebody. Hoping.

And I ended up knowing one person, Danny Rosetti, Ryan Rosetti's uncle. Was a friend of mine, grew up in the neighborhood. And Danny was a construction guy. He had a two day job on like the ninety-ninth floor of the World Trade Center. So they were able to find his body

Sorace: I worked at the World Trade Center with the USAR team. My assignment then on the team was a rescue specialist. We went out and just searched all kinds of places. Searched places and dug here and dug there and we'd find stuff, find bodies and stuff. I don't know how you'd log everything. We worked our twelve hour shifts, searching in buildings that were damaged and on the rubble pile. My first assignment we were literally digging, tunneling straight down through the pile. Then before we ended up getting to the bottom, we literally had to cut through the firetruck to get underneath it. Just as we're getting through it my crew was relieved by another crew, some New York guys who took our spot. That was real, real early in the stage and we had already worked for many, many, many hours, so it was time for us to take a break. The USAR is like a fine tuned thing. You have to take your breaks. You have to rehab. So our time was up and we went back. We did our stuff and then we got sent back out again.

What we were involved with was tunneling and tunneling and digging through, going through buildings that were collapsed or were damaged from the collapse of other buildings that landed on them. We're going through them. It was all shoring up some buildings. There was a big I-beam that was just hanging there, so anchoring that so it wouldn't cause any more damage.

We were still in rescue mode. I don't know if we really ever got out of rescue mode. There were people, I believe that were recovered way, way later. So I would say we never really had the mind set of being out of rescue mode.

We worked ten days, twelve hour shifts for ten days. We went into the city and set up our base camp which is a bunch of tents. We set up one of the tents as the command tent and we set up all of our base camp, our base of operations. Some guys went right out to work. Some of the management people went out and talked to the people running the incident. What needed to be done? This is what we have. What do you need? A lot of it was planning and stuff. When we did end up finally going to work, we would generally work from seven in the morning to seven at night then we would switch out. There was a secondary collapse of the one building that was burning. And there were reports of fire companies in there working when it collapsed, but fortunately there was no one in it.

Perdon: Now we get to the pile and we go to the top. I just keep working my way toward the top. We get to the top of the mound. We're up there with New York and there were construction workers all over the place. You really got caught up in the whole scene, the whole situation because everybody was just working with everybody. So, we get to the top. A New York chief comes up; he introduces himself. He says, "These are your guys. You're in charge of them. You take care of them." "Fine," I says. We wind up grabbing lines, working hand lines and while that's happening this old timer comes up to me, he had the rubber coat on. I swear to God. He goes, "Would you please come with me. I found this void and it's big. It looks good." I said, "Fine." So, he goes down in. The guy's an old man. I find out later he's been retired ten years. I can't even go all the way down because it only branched off a little bit. We had to go through a narrow hole to start off with and then it rounded out. As we got about ten feet down in the void it rounded out to where I could sit up. He went up a little bit this way and you could see down now. The void went down this way. He said, "There's a lot of void here." So, we come back out. We go find that Chief who I had spoken to previously. He says, "Well, what do you think?" He's looking at me.

I says, "I think it had legs. I think it's pretty good. It's something that we should check out." So, he winds up calling FEMA and they send up one guy. Well, you know what it was, I'm figuring later on, they send up one guy because they're probably getting calls all over and they wanted to see. If it was worth it then they would call other people. So, he goes down. He turns around to me. He says, "Would you come with me?" So, I go back down. Now he gets to that area where the other guy is. He looks down and he sends his camera down. It goes into this big shaft. It was an elevator shaft and went as far as he could see down. He said, "It just looks like it opens up into a garage down at the bottom." It still had three good walls and he said it opened to a big void at the bottom. That's possibly a garage area. I think he said it might have been about fifty feet down. So, we come back up now. He said, "Well, I'm going to have to get more people, some stuff here." But what comes up is one guy, one other guy from this Ohio FEMA team, it turned out to be. He comes with one other guy. He brings some tools up and he turns around. They look at me. They go, "I guess you want to go, right?" I says, "Sure, absolutely." So, we go back down. Now, I remember he's trying to work his way, the one guy, he's working his way down that one void that's on a sixty degree pitch that leads to the shaft. The guy's holding his feet. I'm holding the guy's feet behind him as he's trying to cut through this piece of metal. If we can get by that, then we rope down and we'll be able to check out that big void at the bottom. But you couldn't get past that piece of metal. He couldn't cut it. He's turning all over trying to but he just couldn't get by. But there were different things. He would move a piece here and another piece of pipe would come down on you. I remember getting hit in the chest with a piece of pipe. You could actually see there was a piece of rebar that he tried to move. As he moved it, he could see things would just shift, big pieces of concrete and stuff. He says, "All right we're going to leave that in place there." But things were just moving in on you. Things could happen just like that. We wind up getting out of there, but that's where the funny part of the story begins. So, now we're out of there. We were in there for quite a while. I go up to the Chief. I said, "Listen, we're going to go down, take a break." He says, "Go right ahead." He says, "You guys did good. You deserve it."

We're going down the hill and all of the sudden we, the guys from Ten Engine, hear, "U S A. The U S A." The whole place erupts in this, a couple of thousand people. They all start chanting U S A. We're going down the hill. I'm looking around. I'm going, "What's up." We wind up asking this one guy. He says, "They just rescued some guys from Chicago or someplace." So, I'm like "Really." It's like I almost had tears in my eyes because I'm so happy. But as we get down somehow the story got out that it was us. That we were in a hole. That we were trapped. So, they wind up stopping Paul Bartelloni. They ask him, "Could we help you take your coat off?" Paul says, "Oh, yeah. Help me take my coat off." Danny Farrell and I are laughing at him. So, we're going, "Look at Paul." But what it was, they thought he was down in the hole. He had a Ten Engine shield on. Ten Engine from the fire department, New York, they were right there. So, they all thought he was there and he was one of the rescued guys.

All of the sudden the crowd just swarmed on Danny and I. And that's when all the focus was on us. Like we were the guys rescued, just one thing led to the other. The two guys from Ohio were there. These people want to talk to me. They want my name. They want all this stuff. I'm saying, "Wait a minute. Don't bother me. I'm not the person. Talk to these guys from Ohio." And I'm trying to walk away. They're saying, "We want your name." I said, "Well, you're not getting it." They're following me and I'm waving them off. If you ever see that clip they had on TV, they got me going like this. I'm saying, "Get the fuck out of here." So, the guys from Ohio take me to their staging area just to get me out of there. I hang around with them for a little bit and then I leave. They were waiting for me. They were going, "There he is." And Danny Farrell is laughing his ass off. I don't want to be bothered. So, these big wigs from the New York City Police Department come up to me. They're introducing themselves. I'm like shaking their hands, just about looking at them because I'm embarrassed by the whole thing. I mean, here's New York, they took a hit like you couldn't believe. There should be no focus on us at all, period. I felt bad about the whole situation.

I see the old guy, the old New York fireman. He comes up. Now he's making it worse. He's coming. He goes, "Hey you, you were ballsy. You were hell on wheels." He's going. I'm like, "Shut the fuck up!" They're just feeding on that now, the other people. The big wigs from the Police Department, "Here I want you to meet this guy, this clergy." And I'm not paying attention to who it was. I just kind of "Yeah, all right. Nice to meet you." Didn't even look. Danny Farrell goes to me, he goes, "Do you know what you just did?" "What are you talking about?" He goes, "Here's how it works. It's God, the Pope, and him." It was Cardinal Egan. It was Cardinal Egan. I nixed him off. I was just embarrassed by the whole situation. I shouldn't have been the focus of anything. But I wound up seeing the Cardinal walk by later and now I'm going, "Hey Cardinal." Like he's my old friend. I introduced him to Danny. I patted him on the back. When he walked away, his black jacket, all you see was my handprints on his back. I come home. We're coming back to the firehouse and as soon as I get there Ten Engine is like, "What are you nuts?" They made a tape all ready for me. I felt awful it was on the TV. They got blown out of proportion there big time.

I wish I could have done more. I wish we could have gotten down there to get a good look. It wasn't in the cards. I tell you I had to respect everything those guys from FEMA did. I felt, as hairy as it was, you felt kind of safe being with them. Very professional, very knowledgeable. They were checking the air for C O levels and all this other shit. It was an experience. I wish we could have done something better, but that wasn't in the cards.

What I wound up finding out though was the film that was given to all these news agencies. I remember seeing this one guy there. He was in fire department gear. He had a camera. He had a video camera. He was the guy I was trying to run away from as I went around the truck. If you ever see the clip, I'm going around trying to get away from him. And he's running following me. What he was doing was selling this; he was just going around taking pictures and selling it to news agencies. He happened to be there and I was there too. That's how it got to the extent that it did. My wife saw him on another show. He was talking about it. He had people taking pictures of him every place of importance at that scene. He was just one of those guys looking to capitalize on the situation money wise most likely.

But as far as being at that scene, as ugly as it was it was a lot of beauty there. Just the way people worked together. There really was no worry about black, white. You shared water with anybody who would share water with you. You didn't want for anything. Not a Goddamn thing. If you wanted a pair of socks, they gave you a pair of socks. The food, it was there. They would just bring water up to you. But the way people were working with each other, the construction workers, hand in hand, side by side. I mean as soon as we got there, we found a body. I mean it was right there. They were still cutting it out when we left. It was a woman. But everybody was working side by side.

Farrell: It was really a surreal, surreal, surreal, I'll say it one more time, surreal experience, but it's sweet also. Just walking to it, if you didn't know Manhattan, you would have thought you were in a dream sequence. There was dust; you didn't have a good perception of where you were because things were just so covered. We're walking blocks to the site. I can remember people on the side cheering. You were like a god at that point. Didn't affect me much. I remember walking in the street. You hear them. You hear the people. You hear what they're saying and you appreciate that. I remember being so focused going, what is this going to look like when I turn this corner. We turned the corner right underneath that walkover, that trestle and it was like holy cow. Bang. Whoa. And George being George goes right to the pile. He starts climbing up the pile. There's a bucket brigade there and we walked by all these people. I'm looking back at Pauly going, "Where's he going?" Who are we? We're nobodies, you know what I mean. We're a fire department from across the river. Here are all these FDNY guys and we're passing everybody. We got to the top of the pile, the top of the pile. They stretched a line up. It landed in my lap. I looked at George. George looked at me. I said, "Let's go." We're putting out spot fires for hours. Then the FEMA guys were there, who are unbelievable by the way. They're walking around. At one point they were going around to all the little void spaces because they knew there were elevator voids. There were all kinds of voids and they were looking for life. It was only a day later so it was still search and rescue. George went with them at one point. There was a narrow hole. Two guys went down. I was lowering them all down. George went down. I'm thinking I'm going with my captain here. I go to go down the hole. He's doing this to me. What? Stay right there. I stayed by the hole. They did what they had to do.

Now I pulled all three of them out of there. I said to George, "Not for nothing, but I don't want you going into that hole without me. I mean, we're kind of a company, we kind of stay together." "Not for nothing Danny, you weren't fitting in that hole." "Wow, it wasn't that small." "It was a small enough hole. I don't think you were fitting in that hole," he said.

But coming off the pile was probably the most amazing experience, just being there. The greatest bittersweet experience of my life other than my father passing was the fact that you come off this pile and all this horrific stuff that went on. Then you look around and you take a different aspect. You look around and you see the thousands up on the pile. We're working next to firemen from Germany, France, got FEMA guys from all over the country. There were firemen from everywhere, California. There were firemen all over the place and the people that couldn't get on the pile and do that.

Now the bucket brigade, it gave people a sense of I'm doing something. You were taking five gallon buckets and there were thousands of them. You were just piling stuff into them and passing them down. Really? That big of a pile, you're going to do anything with. But it didn't matter. They were contributing and they had to contribute. There were people there, what can I do? What can I do? There were ladies and other guys, different companies just laying out food. Coming off the pile, they're taking the jacket off, putting cold compresses on you. Water, what can I get for you honey? Lead you over. Let me feed you. Washing your feet. It was unbelievable. There was so much good will around that bad scene, amazing good stuff around an amazing bad thing. It was really an amazing place and we were there for four days. We happened to be there the last day where they went from search and rescue to search and recovery. They called off the search and said no one could be surviving now. That wasn't exactly four days later. We were there four times, probably over the course of a week maybe, a week or so within our schedule. It was unbelievable.

As a matter of fact, the first time off the pile they thought we saved somebody. Earlier that morning they had some rescue guys trapped and as we're coming off the pile these guys got saved. No one could tell who did what, but they saw us coming off the pile at that point and they thought it was us. Now the news crews are following us around and they're grabbing for us and they're cheering us. Then we realized what they're doing and we're going, "No, you got the wrong people." They kept going after George Perdon and Perdon's going, "No, you got the wrong guy." Even on the news you could see him. "You got the wrong guy. It's not me. It's somebody else." They didn't care. They just wanted to cheer something, you know.

Now we're off the pile and this is when they think that we were the guys that saved the other guy. The word still didn't get out properly that it wasn't us. We're sitting there and George is talking to one of the captains or chiefs from FDNY. Here comes Cardinal Egan walking over. I know who this guy is. I'm watching him walk over. I go, "George look." Egan comes over with his entourage. "Thank you so much for what you did. And I really appreciate it." George said to him, "Yeah thanks." And he turns around and completely ignores him, starts talking to the guy from FDNY. Well, Egan kind of shrugged his shoulders and turned and walked away.

I went up to George. "George, what are you doing?" "What I was in the middle of a conversation." I said, "Do you have any idea who that guy was?" "No." "That was Cardinal Egan," I said, "in the Catholic faith it goes, God, the Pope, and then this guy and you pissed him off." "You think I should say something?" "Yes, go." George went up to him, had a nice conversation. I wasn't part of it but I saw him walk off. He said he apologized to him. He said, "I'm sorry I didn't know who you were." He goes, "No, no, no, no." Cardinal Egan was really cool about it. Really nice man. Just a regular guy. I mean if he came in civilian clothes, he's a regular guy. You could sit down and have a beer with him. He's just a regular guy. It was an unbelievable experience, it really was.

Bartelloni: George Perdon was my captain. George was one of the most aggressive guys you're ever going to run into. I remember him speaking to a chief in the FDNY. The chief basically told him, "Listen, there's too much going on here. You manage your people and you supervise them." George was just, "I have no problem with that." We grabbed a hoseline and we went pretty much right to the top of the pile and worked on the pile for a while. Then I know they had the urban search and rescue I think from Chicago, where they were trying to check shafts. George had crawled into a hole, went with them. We maintained pretty much trying to put out hot spots while they were keeping fires down that day. There was a lot of smoke. We had little spackle masks that they gave us because you couldn't use air tanks. It was impossible, climbing up on the girders and everything. The guys worked hard that day.

I can tell you a funny story about what happened afterwards. This one is one for the ages; we were actually on the news that night. I had come off the pile and we were caked in white powder. I had a number ten on my helmet. So they were looking for some type of miracle. When I came out, there was a sea of people out there, construction workers, there were loads of people. So this guy comes up to me. He says, "Can I help you with your jacket?" We were exhausted. I said, "Sure, absolutely." "Let me give you some water." "Dynamite," I says. We're parched. So, he says, "How'd you get out?" I said, "What? What are you talking about? How did I get out?" Because he's saw Engine Ten. He thought we were one of the people trapped. So then all of the sudden the crowd starts chanting USA,USA. I'm like, "Oh, no. They got this whole thing wrong." Now George is almost chuckling behind me with Danny Farrell. And I'm like, "No, you got, no." They wanted a miracle. They didn't even want to hear it. So then they started to talk to me. George and Danny are chuckling and so I said, "That's my captain. You should get a statement from George Perdon."

So, the Cardinal was there and he came over. He wanted to speak to George. And George is trying to tell him get away. This is out of control. He ends up talking to the Cardinal. He says, "No, we were working. We're from New Jersey, from Newark and we're just helping out and because we have a Ten." I guess they had video crews out there and they started, "They found people." Somebody had clips of it. I never saw it, but it's just a crazy story. They were looking for any ounce of survival, of hope and we were it for a few minutes. So that was our story, but it was a tough day. Everybody worked, everybody worked hard there that day.

I went the first day. I didn't go back. We had some issues with going there. I know the city didn't want you to go out there. They weren't going to cover you. Guys went anyway. We were on top of that pile. I got hit with so much smoke that day with that spackle mask that did nothing for you. My head was pounding. You kind of knew that something wasn't right. Whether it was asbestos or whatever, this was different. I didn't go back, but I know some other guys that did. We didn't. That was pretty much it for us, but it was tough.

It was a tough day for everybody involved, emotional. I know some people really got beat up over it and couldn't get over it, some of the Newark guys. One that worked with me, John Nepa, he was an emotional guy and he was out of whack for a while. Could have used therapy after that. Great man really. Wore his heart on his sleeve.

Brownlee: It was a mess, really. You weren't ready for that. It was total destruction there. We found a couple of little finger parts. It wasn't a good time. The high point was on the Friday. Georgie Perdon fell in a hole and everybody thought he was a fireman that they found. They brought him up to Cardinal Egan and the Cardinal kept saying, "God bless you." And George kept saying, "I'm not one of them. I'm not one of them." And finally George said, "Fuck you, I ain't one of them." And walked away. That was the high point of the whole trip.

I was really impressed with the dogs over there. The search dogs, they were unbelievable. I was down in a hole. I don't know how deep I was and I hear behind me (sound of a dog panting). I look and it's this German Shepard that I think is going to crew my butt off. He just squeezes by me and he starts digging in the front, found a little finger.

Partridge: When I first laid eyes on the thing, I remember my first two thoughts. My first thought was this smells like a gigantic car fire. You could also smell death, bodies, and all that sort of thing, but aside from that it smelled like a gigantic car fire. My second thought was this is the world's all time worst haz-mat incident. And it certainly turned out to be. Because we were part of the haz-mat unit and had all the training and everything. I guess my mind was trained to think about that kind of thing right away at any kind of incident. We went to work. I was amazed by the dimensions, the proportions of the disaster. I've never seen any pictures or TV coverage that did it justice. I know everybody says that, but it's absolutely true. I had never seen structural steel of those dimensions in my life. Then to see them twisted, mangled, broken was almost beyond comprehension. The piles of debris were huge. Some of them were taller than most buildings in Newark. It was just incredible to take in the magnitude of it. I'll never forget that, just the magnitude of the thing and how small I felt in comparison. All the people that were in there working. It just seemed like ants on an ant hill. That was my impression. They had bucket brigades going. They had guys cutting metal. They had different types of operations going all over the place.

We alternated back and forth. There were times we were on bucket lines because they were trying to rotate people on and off the bucket lines. That's pretty arduous work. But a lot of the time we were searching because we had the training for that being a rescue company. We had rope with us; we had tools with us. We were actually able to get into some of the void spaces and look for people. There were a couple of cases where our guys actually roped into some real deep voids and got a good look around. Then we also got involved with some of the crews that were trying to cut metal and remove heavy debris and that sort of thing. We did an awful lot of actually rescue work there as opposed to just manual labor because we had the training for it. That's what they were really looking for was trained rescue people.

I remember one of my impressions was that this is like a moon scape. Everything just gray everywhere. Everything, the whole entire world was gray like the photos of the moon that we had seen. The other impression that I had was that I had never seen so much paper in my life. There was paper everywhere, paper, paper, paper. Beyond the paper, I don't think I saw anything that was in one piece, anything, whether it was part of the building or part of the contents. There wasn't a telephone; there wasn't a computer; there wasn't a chair, a desk, nothing was in one piece. Everything was somehow broken to different degrees. And then when it came to the human remains that we found, still the same thing was true. Nobody was in one piece. It was to different degrees; they were in bigger or smaller pieces, but they were in pieces. It seemed to me it was like a gigantic blender when the buildings collapsed. The force was incredible and it must have been the loudest noise in the history of the world for those who were there. It was just incredible to take it in. When we were there, there were a couple times when they thought they had found people. It always turned out that they hadn't, that they heard some noise or they had some clue that they thought was someone. Then they would sound a signal that meant everybody was supposed to be quiet all over the pile. So they could hear if anybody was trying to yell for help or something like that. And it never turned out while I was there that they found anybody. As we all know after the fact, very few people were pulled out alive even on the first day, even within the first twenty-four hours. There were also a couple of times when they sounded an alert that meant we were supposed to clear the site because they were anticipating another collapse. By this time it had been raining a little bit too, so this gray ash had turned into a kind of very slippery slug. It was as bad as ice if you were trying to walk on the steel. And in a lot of cases you couldn't climb up anywhere without having some kind of rope to latch onto and pull yourself up. I remember thinking, if there's really going to be a collapse nobody's getting out of the way. Nobody's going to be able to move out of the way in time. So they would sound these alarms and we would all start trying to walk off the pile and get back to an area of refuge. Nothing came down, maybe a couple of pieces of steel here or there, but if there had been another major collapse you would have lost another couple of hundred people. Nobody would have been able to get out of the way. It was just too treacherous to move quickly there.

Actually found a fire engine. And the funny thing is up until that point I thought we were operating at street level. This is how massive the debris was and how you really couldn't get a handle as to what was going on. I actually thought we were operating at street level. But this was one of the times when we were trying to cut metal and move stuff and really dig into debris. And it was like, what's that? I start moving stuff and I see diamond plate. Start moving a little more and I see more diamond plate. We got a fire engine here. I send out the word. "Hey, guys we got a rig over here." If you found a fire engine the immediate thought was maybe there's somebody alive in it or under it. Hopefully guys had tried to dive underneath for shelter or get into the cab or something. So as soon as I said we got a fire engine here, FDNY just descended on the thing. Within like an hour we had it uncovered. It was a rear mount aerial. I forget which company it was. An entire rear mount aerial buried to the point where you couldn't see it. We had to dig to find it. I thought we were at street level and then I realized if I'm standing on top of a rear mount, I'm twelve feet up in the air. So that's pretty much what it was like as far as operating on the pile.

You know there were lighter moments, too. I mean one day we were walking into the pile and there was this table where there were these three or four women sitting there offering counseling. They were all pretty good looking women and I had all these guys from Rescue. They approached us to ask if we wanted to talk about anything. And my only thought was uh-oh this is not going to turn out well and I was right. My guys didn't let me down on that one. They were Newark firefighters through and through. In fact by the end of it all a couple of phone numbers had been exchanged. But there were a few lighter moments and times when we were able to laugh about things. That's always going to be true on our job. No matter how horrible something is, you're always going to find something to laugh about to break the tension. And keep everybody on a level plane.

McGovern: The Incident Command system was pretty much set up by then. They were pretty well organized. They had all their equipment lined up and logistics seemed to be getting into place by that time, lot of people there, a big mess. There we hooked up with Sacramento USAR team who were there searching for two days already. We gave them a little break.

We searched, went into the subway. The subway was full of water right up to the top of the subway cars. We broke into a couple of token booths to see if anybody was in there unconscious. We never found anybody.

We were searching tunnels where you couldn't walk. You know, you had to crawl through all that dust. Oh, it was awful. I had a sore throat for a week. We were all over the pile and we went into some of the buildings that were still burning just for a quick look before they ordered us out of there. One was burning pretty good. It was still burning when we got there. The fire was coming out of the windows. We just went up there to take a look around. We didn't have any hose lines. We didn't have any equipment other than our bunker gear. So there wasn't much we could do.

They gave us paper masks. They became pretty much useless with all that sweating. They became clogged, so most of the guys didn't even wear them. At least our guys, I don't know about the others. The USAR team, they had the regular filter masks. We worked there probably until about seven thirty at night before we were ordered back. Got back to the firehouse around I guess around eight o'clock, nine o'clock at night.

Jackson: That was an eerie, eerie moment over there, seeing all that destruction up close and personal. We checked in at the command post and he had us standing by. There were so many companies there. They were so overwhelmed. We actually saw Donald Trump over there too. He came to the scene. He had a bunch of body guards around him. I'm trying to think. Did he fly in? I'm not sure. I could have sworn something about a helicopter or something being there.

We didn't really work. We went to one building and we did a search. We opened up a grate and you could actually see the subway down there. It was flooded. When we were leaving the building, we actually saw this firefighter. He was on a golf cart and he went to a rig. It was a rig that was parked there on the side and still connected to the stand pipe connection. It wasn't in bad shape, but the apparatus was dusty. He went in there, got his shoes on, came out. Somebody asked him something and he said he lost his whole crew. He was the driver.

He was most likely the most junior person too. He was pretty young and he had lost his whole crew. He came back I guess to get whatever personal effects he may have had in the apparatus. That had to be heart wrenching, to be in a situation like that. Because he was driving that day, he survived.

A lot of sad moments over there, but you could still hear music from this little courtyard. It was encased in glass and it separated the two buildings. I guess you could walk from one building to the other, but inside there, there was some music that was still playing. Then right outside there, there are refrigerated tractor trailers. That's where they were putting the firemen. It was eerie. There were piles and piles, I mean six, seven stories high of debris. Metal. Twisted metal, concrete and whenever you would hear, "It's going to fall" everybody would just start running because they were unsure about the stability of the building. They had different people watching out. If you saw the building shift or if you saw something was going to fall they would sound the alarm. Everybody would run from the building. I mean mobs of people just running. Then they'd stand there for a little while until they would get the order to go back. And everybody goes back on the mound.

Serious, I mean dust inches thick. You were kicking through it like you're on the beach. We had the paper masks that you wore. Some people had respirators but a lot of people didn't have anything because the EPA said it was okay. Said the atmosphere was fine, but it wasn't. It was unhealthy.

Greene: We got to the World Trade Center and we really just didn't do a whole lot. We were assisting with search, but someone had searched the area already. The way that place came down, it was always good to have more than one set of eyes go over a location. It was pretty chaotic. It was organized; it was good; but it was chaos still.

It looked unbelievable. That had been a place that I had been to on multiple occasions and you couldn't really recognize anything. It was just bare steel and disintegration. You would think that a building like that with all the telephones or something like that. Something that you could easily identify, you would just be able to pick one up, but everything was disintegrated. It was like a powder.

We weren't on the pile. That was not the area that we went. I believe we were in the remains of either building Six or Seven. It was not the main tower, number one or two. We were searching, but there was nothing to be found. We were ordered up later that evening. And we came back. I believe it was ourselves and Chief McGovern.

Montalvo: We spent the whole day over there just helping dig out. It wasn't a pretty sight. The most I can take from those two days that I spent over there, there was a certain smell that was in the air. What I found out later was those are pretty much the body parts and the bodies decaying. That's one of the only ways that we could tell when we were close to something. There was a certain stench that kept coming out. I remember that day that we were there digging for like three hours underneath the sidewalk and going down. It just kept getting stronger and stronger. I remember right before we left, at that point we were getting ready to leave. There was a head that was stuck on a beam and that's all there was. That's what you're smelling. You're not going to find whole bodies. You're just going to find parts all over, now you start finding an ear here, a finger here. It wasn't pretty at all.

Castelluccio: I never saw destruction like that in my life. It was hard to imagine that you had steel all over the place. Just concrete piled eight, ten stories high. You were like, this was a hundred and ten story building and here we are with buckets going through stuff. You're pulling up business cards from people on the hundred and fourth floor. That was tough.

Weidele: I think it was the second day. I went with Joe Sperli, Chief Spann, and I can't remember, but we went for the whole day. We stayed there. We dug. We cleaned. We did everything we could and then we went home. I went the next two days. One day I met Chief Killeen. I didn't go with him I met him. We did a lot of searching with a couple of other men. John Agoston I remember being there. It was just sad to see something like that happen.

Masters: We went the next night. It was so eerie. It was just walking into a ghost town. You had to look at your feet and it was like ashes covering your ankles. You thought you were in a snowdrift. And the smell, I'll never forget that smell.

It was my crew at Eleven Truck. It was Captain Krutulis, myself, Mike Litterio, Jimmy Costa. Engine Eleven went, the Guidas. Deputy Chief Smith went with us, Jimmy Smith. He asked me if he could borrow a helmet, so I gave him Johnny Griggs' helmet with his permission. I was calling him Griggs all night and he was laughing. I had the privilege of working with Charlie Krutulis in my section. This is the night after the towers fell.

Chief Smith was like a tunnel rat. We had to hold him. It was just tremendous. A tremendous experience, but in the far part it was a very sad experience because you wouldn't find too much left. We went early and we stayed to daybreak and the next night too. I remember our taking a break. We went across the street to Engine Ten and Ladder Ten in New York. They were first due there and their house was a mess, filled with debris. That was like a triage center. You get your stuff off. You get rehab. You talk with some of the New York firemen who just thanked us. They were tremendous. State Police, New York, everybody was great with us.

Sperli: When we were on the bucket brigade, I'm on my hands and knees digging, putting the stuff in the bucket. We're passing it to other people and it's just like so many mixed emotions going on there. You're angry. You're sad. You're horrified. You're in disbelief. And in some way you're hoping that you could find someone in a void space that was still alive, but as it was nobody was ever found, just people's remains. So whatever remains that we found or even personal belongings I now think about and realize that that might be the only thing that the family member had.

If you found an ID card, they had a tent set up. One area was airplane parts. Another area was body parts. And another area was any kind of ID or rings or anything that was personal belongings, purses, wallets, whatever. So if I found like an ID card then I put in there. Because some people were never identified, that might have been the only thing that a loved one had. So in a way I felt, "Oh I didn't find anybody alive." I felt it was kind of a failure on my part, but now I realize that I gave closure to somebody maybe by the things I did find, so. Very frustrating.

Griggs: It was tough, heartbreaking to see all of that. It was hard to really grasp. When I was there it was two mornings after. I remember seeing one fireman just blocks away sitting on a stoop. He was just sitting there. I'm sure he had friends and co-workers that perished or that were unaccounted for. It was just heartbreaking really, just tough to see that.

Lee: So basically we reported to the Command Post and they had us stand by, stand by. As far as physically digging, I did not physically dig at the World Trade Center.

Ostertag: It was a mess. It was like a movie scene. It was surreal. The rubble, body parts, crushed fire trucks, personal belongings, it was crazy. It was weird. You see people's business cards when going through the rubble. And it was like a bucket brigade, it was ancient. But that's what you have to operate under. Fill up buckets, pass it down the line. We were on that pile just seeing pictures of families, pictures of kids, like wow. That was very memorable. We only went that one day because they had enough help, so you know we never went back after that. I spent the whole day there.

That's when we were looking for survivors. That's why when we were on the pile, carefully removing all that debris, every time somebody thought they heard somebody, they would yell out whoa, whoa, whoa, whoa. And it would just go quiet and listen. And there'd be total silence.

Pierre: It was devastating. I've been to Lebanon during the war and I'm looking at Manhattan. I just said, "Oh my God, this is Lebanon." Because everything was so destroyed. You didn't know what you were looking at. All you could see were pieces of buildings here, pieces of buildings there, wires, big steel beams hanging. We went there for a few days. We helped move a lot of stuff, a lot of like stones and stuff like that. I went back to work. I never went back because they were saying, "We don't want anyone else because it's getting too cluttered." All the people coming in from everywhere, so I never went back after that.

Meier: That Friday we spent digging on the pile. So it was really just body parts and death at that point. There were really no salvageable victims. I just spent one day going over the pile.

Burkhardt: They staged us. I think they decided they were going to handle it all by themselves and I probably agree with them. I think at that point it was a recovery thing. You could see where they kind of handled you. They asked you where you were from and they said, "Well stand over there." You could see the deputies were just blowing you off. They had nowhere else to put you and they weren't going to use you. Then like typical firemen, you try to sneak in the backdoor. A couple of us got in for a short period of time. As soon as the Safety Officer would come around and say, "You guys aren't New York, out." Jersey City got to play. I guess they have a good relationship with them. We don't. We don't do well with other departments.

Zieser: We went over there a couple of times. We were working the day of the World Trade Center and I was in a talk with my brothers. They were going to go over that night and I was all set to go. Guys were coming back already, I think it was Frank Bellina and that crew. They already were over there. We're getting ready to go over. Now it's about seven o'clock at night. We got off at six and we were going to go over at seven. Everyone's coming back, there's nothing to do. There's nothing in place, so I didn't go over that first night. A lot of our guys went over the first night and they said they came back for the same reason. There was nothing in place.

The union said they would pay for a bus. We went over there and worked the pile, but at that time it was a little more organized. When they had a command post set up.

LaPenta: It makes you wonder; sometimes people say, "Oh, my father or my grandfather never talked about the war." I know. I get it. Two thousand and one I realized this is why my grandparents never talked about World War II and Korea, because they don't want to talk about it. I get it.

It was crazy. We did more and more and more, I'm not getting into detail. Everybody knows the story. My thought on that was no person should have to experience this and I don't ever want to experience it again. To be quite honest with you, I don't really talk much about it. It gives you nightmares to this day. Seeing the shit that we saw and doing the stuff that we did. I almost died like four times in a week from either buildings falling on us or slipping off an I-beam and falling, falling into where? That's not like tripping off the stairs. You're falling thirty forty feet into a void with jagged steel and concrete. The odds are you're going to get hurt or killed. You know, so that's all I got to say about that.

Langenbach: We made a point; the crew that I went over with made a point of going back every year for the anniversary. I can't say it got easier every time, but it got a little better every time. Now I just sit home and watch it and listen to the names. But we haven't been back, my wife and I have not been back and I haven't been back to the museum. I don't know if I can do that yet. I don't think I'll ever be able to do that. We went back, my brother-in-law and sister-in-law, to the new Freedom Tower. I had a hook with somebody from the State Police and got us up into there and took a look at that. I walked around the pool, but as far as going into the museum, I don't think I'm ready for that. I don't think I'll ever be ready for that. And my wife, she definitely said no, never. We went back like maybe two months afterwards. I said, "I got to go back to this one place, just to repay the guy who gave us that gourmet meal when we were working." They had like an observation platform built so people could go up and look at where the Trade Center was. She looked at that and said, "I could never do this again." The smell was still in the air.

Every once in a while it brings back memories. Because the Trade Center, when we went to New York, we would take the PATH into the Trade Center and then go from there. We would do that a lot. I mean we would go there a lot because we both liked the city. To go there that morning and see there's nothing there, just the shell. It's hard to believe.

Bellina: So we go back to the firehouse and we're working our shift and we see they're doing fifteen, ten funerals a day. And I got this bolt at home. So I'm in the firehouse and Agoston goes, "We got to do something." "Well, what can we do?" He says, "Well we got to start going to these funerals." So we started going to funerals in Staten Island and other places but mainly Staten Island. There's a guy, his name is Joe LaPointe. He's a lieutenant. He just got promoted to lieutenant in the New York City fire department. He was in the

Academy at the time being trained to be a lieutenant and they put him in a detail to run all the funerals on Staten Island. Sharp guy, had a flat top, he reminded me of a Marine. So we get involved with him. We were at every funeral. I was organizing trips. The fire department was letting me take a van and I would put out the pictures of the guys that we're going to do that day and a little story about them. I put it in the firehouses and said come with us. We were moving Newark firemen over there. We were definitely twelve, twenty guys, at a time. Agoston and I got to know this guy. He said to me, "Frank we need help. We need a rig from Newark to help us because there are not enough caisson units. It's tradition. Can you get a rig? At least a ladder company, put a flag on it."

I made the pitch to the director and he said, "No way. I'm not doing that." So somebody is involved with a Councilwoman named Gail Chaneyfield. She's got a connection with Sharpe James. She can probably make this happen for you. I didn't give a shit at that point. I mean our country was devastated. These guys were hurting and because the director doesn't want to send equipment over there. Are you out of your mind? So I talk to this lady. She goes, alright let me see if I can get an appointment. She gets an appointment to see Sharpe James. I could get, probably, suspended minimum for what I'm doing. I'm a fireman, breaking the chain of command royally. I can't go much higher than that. I get a meeting, John Agoston and myself, full dress uniform, with Mayor Sharpe James with the Councilwoman. Explain yourself. So I said, "Mr. Mayor, they need these. It's a tradition." "I don't see a problem with this," he says, "Hold on." He calls the Director up. He puts him on speaker phone and says, "Director, I'm sitting here with Firefighters Bellina and Agoston." The Director goes, "Who?" The Mayor goes, "Bellina and Agoston. They're sitting in my office right now and they're requesting a fire truck to go to New York to help with the funerals." The Director goes, "Yes, there was a request. You know how I feel about that, Mr. Mayor. I barely do mutual aid. I don't want to send it into another state." The Mayor says, "Well, you're going to do exactly what they want you to do. It's going to happen." So he's quiet on the other side. "You're going to make this happen. Whatever they want, you're going to make happen. I want this done." "Okay, Mr. Mayor, whatever you want." And being Frank Bellina, idiot that I am, I just can't let things go. I say, "Director, do you want me to call you or you'll call me?" Not being belligerent, but I didn't want the moment to pass. He says, "I'll be in contact with you." Like nasty and hangs up. Okay, I go back to the firehouse, Twelve Engine. It's Martin Luther King holiday. No one's working in the city. I'm sitting on Five Truck's side and we're preparing lunch. Phone rings. "Frank." They got their hand over the phone. "It's the Director. He wants to talk to you." I'm going, "Yeah, okay." "Frank, it's the Director. He wants to talk to you." I get on the phone. I say, "Director, I just want to - --." "No, no whatever you need." Doesn't understand. He thinks I'm hooked major league. Now he's kissing my butt. Seventeen Engine at the time had a brand new apparatus. They just got it. It was a white with blue lettering. "Those guys over at Seventeen, I'm having the hose taken off. They're going to get a spare. You're going to get that truck. They're going to do whatever you need."

So we bring Seventeen Engine over there and we do a couple of funerals with it. The guy was appreciative. We used Seventeen Engine at that first funeral for a flower car. They actually had a caisson that day. So we get that done. Now whatever the guy needs, I'm getting done. He's not asking me for much. Kind of got things under control over in New York.

I'm standing in line one day. We did I don't know how many funerals, John and I. We would go, stand in line and here comes an antique fire truck, right. And it's got New York City on it. We're in line and we're saluting at the time as the casket goes by. I go, "John that's pretty cool. What, do they have antiques?" So he goes, "I'll talk to you when we're done." So we break. And he goes, "No, that's probably somebody's private fire truck." Like an antique and they put New York City magnetic signs on there. They're using it to carry caskets. But New York City has these things which are called caisson units which I've seen. At the time they had one.

I go, "That's something we should have in the city." He goes, "Yeah, but Frank if want to get something, you got to get a B model Mack." Frank, not knowing what a B model Mack is, goes back home. On the internet I search it. Sure enough brings me back to Fifteenth Avenue. B model Mack, frigging fire truck. Yeah I know what that is. I've seen them screaming through the streets. Those were the things that made my stomach turn. Okay. Frank goes on the internet and he's trying to find one. Frank's going to buy one. Frank's going to find a fire truck and we're going to bring that to New York City and we're going to use it. This is Frank's mentality. Okay. So I tell Agoston. "Alright, whatever." I said, "I'm going to find one, alright."

So, obviously I don't find one because the city of Newark lets everything rot. It stays down at the Fire Academy and rots. And then we junk it. It's not even worth scrap because it's rust. So, what Frank does is Frank researches and finds a book written about B model Macks from this guy Harvey Elsner. Well, Frank being Frank, I get the guy's name. He's from Wisconsin. It gives the town, but it doesn't say where he lives. I call the police department that's in the town. I say, "Do you know this guy?" They say, "Who are you?" I said, "Newark fire department. We're trying to help New York City." At that time, if you said anything about New York City, you were trying to help them, they didn't care. Guy goes, 'Hold on." Gives me his phone number, unlisted phone number. Gives me the phone number of the guy that wrote the book. I call the guy up at home. He goes, "How did you get my number?" And I tell him, "Look put that aside. This is what I'm doing." He's all on board with me. He goes, "Listen I got all the serial numbers. I'll tell you right now, there's nothing in Newark. There's nothing left from Newark. There's no Newark apparatus out there. There's none. But there's a B model Mack on Ebay being auctioned off right now. I know, three guys. They're friends of mine that are bidding on this. Lucent went out of business and this company is doing the liquidation of it. They're bidding on it. They want, I think it was twenty thousand or twenty-five thousand for this apparatus, but it's only got five thousand miles on it. If you want it then I'll have these guys back off of it and they won't bid on it." Frank being Frank says, "I want it." You're talking between twenty and twenty-five thousand dollars.

I don't have any money. All I got is this idea. So the guy goes, "You got it." I know nothing about Ebay. Well, three or four days go by. The liquidation company calls me up. The guy's screaming at me. "Who hell are you? I'm going to get a lawyer. We're going to sue you. These guys backed off of this. I got your name. You're the cause of this. Who are you to do this?" "Slow down", tell him the story. He goes, "You want the truck? Fifteen thousand it's yours. Okay, but it's in Kentucky." So I says, "I'm taking the truck." I have a meeting with Agoston and maybe ten, twelve other firemen. What do you want to do Frank? I want this truck. Here's the picture of it. Okay, what do you want to do? I want to do New York City funerals. Okay, we're in. What do you want to do? Let's go to the credit union, take out a loan. Took a loan, got fifteen thousand dollars. Got Chief Nasta, owned a trucking company. Chief can you pick this up for us? Not a problem Frank. He rents a low boy, you know, with a trailer truck, goes out there. I give him the fifteen thousand. He goes out there. I said, Chief don't give him anything until you call me. Looked it over then called me on his cell phone. I want to see if I can get him down from fifteen thousand. Nasta's out there. I hear him open compartment doors. "Frank, this thing is beautiful. This thing's like crazy. It's untouched." I says, "See if you can get ten thousand." Me, I don't talk softly. The guy hears it on the other end. He goes, "I'm going to tell you right now, you give me the fifteen or get the hell out of here." I go, "Give him the fifteen thousand." So he gives him the fifteen thousand dollars. He puts it on the truck and brings it back to Newark.

Within two days we figured out that we can use a motorcycle lift that works on one of our air bottles to raise the casket up. We retrofit it. Bobby Carter, Jimmy Weiss, myself, and other people. We weld on the back of this truck. We know nothing about this truck. We don't know if it's going to explode. We get it lettered Newark Fire Department. We bring it over there and do I don't know how many funerals with it.

That's where the bolt goes. Now it all makes sense. The bolt goes on the dashboard of the Mack. We built the Mack around that frigging bolt. That's where the bolt went. It got glued on the dashboard. To this day it's down there. One of the coolest stories ever was we were asked to do the funeral of a firefighter that lived in New Jersey. He was killed at the Trade Center. They found his remains. Because we were in New Jersey, the guy LaPointe called me and said can you do the casket. Absolutely, so we did this funeral at a place in Somerset from the funeral home to the church. All took place in New Jersey and they buried him in New Jersey.

Little did I know there was a battalion chief that was there from New York City. His son, just came out of the Academy, was killed. Now this battalion chief's still on the job in New York City, his son was killed. The last name was Richardson. His son was killed in the World Trade Center. He sees the truck and he makes a request to LaPointe. At the time they had two caisson units working in New

York. They were available. They were slowing down. They were only doing maybe two funerals a day or one a day when they were finding remains. The father says, "I don't want the New York City caisson unit, I want this one from Newark. I saw what they did and I want that for my son." Guy goes, "I got a special request Frank. Battalion chief, his son was killed, just got out of the Academy, World Trade Center, but it's in Brooklyn. You got to go to Brooklyn, to the funeral home and it's going to go to St. Patrick's Cathedral. So, it was like two degrees. We rode the rig with the casket down to St. Patrick's Cathedral. They made a sign over Newark. It said New York City. You never knew it was a Newark rig. Well, it was never really a Newark rig, but kind of by default, but here we are. St. Patrick's Cathedral, asked to do this.

There's more to it, there's a lot more that happened but that to me was the ultimate. To know that we did that. I didn't have the nerve to drive it. Danny Prachar would drive it because he was familiar with those rigs and he would drive it. I didn't want to take a chance of driving it. Then we were asked to do one in the South Bronx. It was like one of the last firefighters that they found. They did the same thing. And the City of New York got pissed off said, "No we're available. We're doing it." Von Essen at the time was the Commissioner. This particular firehouse in the South Bronx was where he was from. They were pissed the way New York City was handling the whole thing over there, the World Trade Center. The firemen said we want that fire truck from Newark to carry his casket. Von Essen got involved. He said, "They're using that truck. That's the end of it. That's the truck they're using." Again we did the funeral there. It was one of the last ones. This guy Buhl I think his last name was. So we had the honor of doing that.

Killeen: It's very hard. It's really, really hard. Part of it is that my daughter was really upset. I put her under a lot of duress and I never thought about it until that night. I'm sure I put my wife under a lot of duress, but she never talked about it. But other parts of it, I find it really hard. I can't watch any documentaries about it. It's like, "Whoa I can't take it." You're the only person that I talked to that hasn't been there that I can talk about it. It's one of those things. I can talk to you. I can talk to you about a lot of things, but not to anybody else. Some people like Agoston I can talk to, Sigano, because they were there and the things click. But other than that I just can't talk to anybody else about that.

I put it into a box in the back of my mind. That's one of those boxes, you know, you have some bad nights at work, some bad deaths, and that's in that box. And this is in its own box.

Richardson: I remember seeing the pictures of guys; they're standing on the pile taking a picture. You know it just burned me up. My picture was taken. I know my picture was taken because I saw the guy take my picture. I don't have a copy of that picture. Besides the people that went that day and my family knowing, there is no record of me ever being there. There might be a couple of pictures in somebody's locker that maybe someday somebody will look at and say, "Who the heck is this guy?" But I didn't take a picture to memorialize and say, "Oh, I was there. I was there." You don't believe me that I was there. Then I really don't care. That's not why I went. And it burned me up when you saw so many pictures out there. Not just Newark guys, but guys from all different departments taking a picture on this fucking pile. Are you kidding me?

But yeah it was emotionally very, very difficult. I was there for the one day. I can say that I was. But that was about it. I mean, am I proud to say, "Yeah I was the first group with Frank Bellina and Kevin Killeen over there?" I was just with a group of guys that went over there. Mike Sorace was there for more than a week. I think his throat cancer was because of that. I don't quite know if it was ever proven to be that, but you know he was there with Task Force One. I give them a lot of credit, those guys.

I don't really care what people call me, but I mean I laid curled up in a bed the next day. It was just so surreal and so mind boggling. I just couldn't do it again. I've never been back. Every time I go into New York, I say I want to go to the memorial. I haven't walked back there. It was a tough time.

Alexander: I mean it's hard to describe because it just set in your mind and it made me realize, "Hey what's going on here? Is the world coming to an end here?" I had never experienced anything like it. But from that it just made me put my job into perspective. What I do. And from there I just want to say that I took that and made myself a better person. Realizing how short life is, it's made me understand my role in this world as a father, as a husband. The things that I have to do to protect my family and the teachings I have to do. So, the World Trade Center was more than just seeing the devastation. It helped me a lot and it bothered me a lot.

You're searching for people. It was whoa, not the stuff I would say you like talking about. You can relate one fireman to another one, you can. But when you try to talk to people outside of it, you can't. It's a thankless job, man.

Straile: To this day I think that's what unfortunately killed Joe D'Alise because he was a digger. He was down in there. I think some of that crap must have really got to him.

Griffith: It's something I'll never ever forget and in fact I did the tunnel to towers run last year. I had gone back a couple of times before that. I'm not a real emotional person, but I went back there with my kids once. There was a school bus trip. I went there and I got very emotional when I got there. A real good friend of mine worked at Cantor Fitzgerald for the commodities exchange. As a matter of fact he actually called my wife that night and said, "Where's Eddie?" She said, "He went over there." He said, "What's he doing going over there?" She said, "He's looking for you and Tommy." "Tell him to get out of there. I'm okay."

But I went back to the tunnel to towers thing. It was mainly because I did what I did with my weight and all of that. It was a goal that I set for myself and these young firemen put it together. They've been doing it for a few years now, young Newark firemen that go over there. It's a nice thing that they're doing. They raise money for charity for that Steven Stiller Foundation. I went there and I got the story of this guys that worked in Brooklyn and couldn't get over there. He actually had his gear, ran through the tunnel, and ultimately paid the ultimate sacrifice. I did the run which is something even a year before there was no way I was walking that let alone run it. I ran it and got through with it. There was so much closure. To see the city in that area where it was fixed and new, then they had videos playing all over, giant screens and video and people talking. It was wow.

We got done with the run and we're walking back. We actually had the fire department pipe band bus. They had some water and stuff there and our personal stuff was on the bus as well. We went back and we're walking through the memorial area which is something I hadn't seen, a really beautiful place. They ran in their gear. I couldn't run in my gear because they're worried about hydration for me. People start asking, "Were you here then? Were you here then?" And I'm listening to these guys and they go, "No, you know, I'm a younger guy." I'm thinking, fourteen years at the time, fourteen years later, a lot of guys that were there that day are retired.

Now I'm listening to these guys tell a story. A lot of these guys were military guys. They were guys that were in the military. Their reason for joining the military was because of this. They grew up, "No, I got to go into the military. I got to deal with this." And then they come out and now they're firemen. I'm saying wow. It was funny to hear because I said, "Oh, I was there that day." And they said, "You were?" I'm looking. Gene Hurley was there. He had been there that day. There were only a few of us. Tony Tarantino was another guy that was there. There were like three of us out of the twenty-one or thirty guys. There were only three of us that had actually been there that day.

So they were talking to us and it was interesting to hear how it impacted them. You think about fourteen years earlier. How old these guys were. They're in their twenties, even thirty. They were fifteen years old. So yeah it was amazing to hear their reasons why they're here. And then there's, "Wow you were here?" Then they're asking questions. "What about this?" I could say well this was here and I was pointing out different things. Their jaws were down, like you were here, wow. I said, "No, no, no. Listen I just happened to be here. It's not that I did anything because anybody that was in my position would do it. You had a hundred and twenty guys and it was even more. It was a hundred and twenty in that particular group. But overall, there was a load of guys that went over there. It was only because you had the proximity to do it that you did do something. That's why you do what you do. So I said, "Don't think of me as special because we all do the same thing." But it was a lot of closure.

After that I came over with my wife for our anniversary. It was a Monday and now the two of us went. We spent the whole day. We did a tour, did the museum and then actually went up to the Freedom Towers, all part of the package. The guy that gave the tour was fantastic. He filled in the blanks. I got him on the side and I tipped him because he did a great job. He tells me stories. He goes, "Were you here?" And I said, "Yeah. I came over. I'm retired from Newark." I said, "Keep doing what you're doing. You're doing an excellent job. Just tell the story." This guy was actually going to school down there and he lived through it.

Then we went down to see the museum. It brought back a lot of things because you see things you saw. There are things that I saw, brought back memories. Wow, it's done in a really fitting way. It's beautiful for the families to have some place to go because in most cases there's no burial. It's a place they can go and reflect. And then what was nice, the building was built back up. It kind of showed, "Hey, to terrorists go ahead, but you know what? We'll come back bigger and stronger."

Then we went up to the top and we did the observatory. It was beautiful. There's actually a bar up there. I said, "Let's go in." And my wife said, "Whoa, I don't know." "No," I said, "Let's go in for our anniversary and salute those people that sacrificed like that. We went in there, sat down and had a glass of wine. Eighteen dollars a glass, but we did that. She said, "That's fitting." It was really nice that we did that. And of course we come down and went to dinner, but that kind of put things in perspective.

It's amazing, such a horrible thing and really people trying and now that whole business area really thriving. Even the neighborhoods, because we stayed overnight and the neighborhoods and the kids growing up down there and the schools. It's really something nice to see. But that's something that I'll never ever forget. Those images are burned in my mind forever. Hope that nobody ever has to go through that, ever, ever on this soil.

Roberson: It's a shame now that we can't get our own congress and government to pass a bill to pay for these guys' medical insurance. They're dying of cancer. All from that incident from breathing all that material and all that dust that got in their lungs, the fire, the police, even the civilians. It's crazy how they won't even help our own people.

West: I went to a handful of funerals. Certainly there were way too many, but I went to a handful. Trying to remember, at the time I had a business. I had a landscaping business on the side. So I really didn't have a lot of free days to go to all of them, but any one that I could I jumped on. I probably went to about maybe six or seven which is really not many compared to how many they actually had. But sometimes, you know, you got to do what you have to do in your personal life with your own business and stuff like that. So, every little bit helps, I guess.

Ironically enough, I have not been to the museum. I don't know. It sort of bothers me, the whole thing, to think about it. My family has. My wife and kids have, but I have not been there. In all these years I haven't really brought myself to go over there. I really should. I was part of it in a small way, but I just haven't really found a way to get myself over there. Just not ready yet. It's just too depressing, quite frankly.

Willis: I didn't go to any of the funerals or memorials. You had guys that would go to all of them. I didn't think it was healthy. I did enough. I didn't want to go. My feelings were different towards that. I didn't want to go. I went to the ceremonies, but I wouldn't go to anyone's funeral. I had enough to deal with in my head. So that's how I felt. I did an interview ten years after with a news channel called Patch or something. They did a big interview with us. Matter of fact, one of the guys that was at almost every funeral, broke down and couldn't do the interview. You can see it took a toll on him. I knew. Something told me, don't go for that reason. I mean I don't want to see people mourning every day. I think they went to fifty or sixty funerals with the caisson unit. I couldn't do it. I think it was more emotional and stressful. Didn't want it, so I avoided it.

But I went to the ceremonies. I would go to any 9/11 ceremony. Ours in Newark or New York, more New York just because it seemed here the administration didn't care. Sharpe James' administration did not care. They told us not to go and then wind up giving awards out to everybody. I wouldn't go. I wouldn't sign my name. I wouldn't give them any information. I wouldn't cooperate with him for the fact that he didn't give two craps about us when we were going over. Why am I going to make him look good? That was one of the main drivers as to why I backed Booker in the Mayor's election. Me, Dave, all of us because he didn't care.

I've been to ground zero many a times while they were building it. My nephew is an iron worker. A lot of my family are iron workers.

I went over while they were building, but I've never been to the memorial at all. I want to and it's not there. I'm not ready yet. I'm not ready. My son's a firefighter now. My nephews are firefighters. There are six of us now in my family, counting my son-in-law. There's a bunch of us. I figure we'll do it as a family when I retire. I want to do it when I retire and that's right around the corner, coming up very shortly.

Right now I'm involved with the 9/11 victims' fund. I went and took physicals. They're working on my case right now. I had throat cancer like all the fireman in New York had. Squamous cell carcinoma, I had it in my throat, inside of my neck. They had to take fifty-six lymph nodes out of my neck. They took my tonsils, about a quarter inch of the roof of my mouth, and part of my throat. I had a robot. A robot did it. The World Trade Center Commision is right now working on certifying me, whether it was caused by 9/11. I can't say for sure. I'm going to say since it's what all the guys are coming down with in New York that they're probably going to side in my favor and say yeah it was.

The last two and a half years have been stressful since the surgery. I'm going in August now again for my PET scan. All of them have been coming up clean. So I thank the surgeons in Morristown Hospital for all they did for me. They saved my life. Hopefully two and a half more years and I'll be declared cancer free. So I'm just waiting on the World Trade Commission. They made an offer. They told me that it's available. All those prescriptions related to my throat cancer will be covered for the rest of my life. And all co-pays relating to my throat and neck as long as I use their doctors, I'll be taken care of for the rest of my life regardless if they deem it 9/11. Because I was there, that's taken care of. I'm hoping that the certification goes through. It's in Washington, D.C. right now. We'll find out. The woman called me and she's optimistic that they're going to accept my case.

I'm not worried about compensation as much as being taken care of. The compensation part, yes, everybody would like to be compensated. I have a wife and children. If anything happens to me, I would like it to go to them and my grandchildren. I'm hoping that they accept it and I'm hoping that I'm around to enjoy life because these doctors did wonders. It was a robot that did this operation. It wasn't a human. I was under for twelve hours. It was a hell of an experience. I have a lot of aftereffects. I have no saliva glands. I have no taste or smell, but I don't complain. I'm grateful. I get to talk about it. At every union meeting I stress to these new guys, even older guys, don't think like we did in the old way we learned from the guys from the seventies. I had Billy Melodic with me. Those guys didn't wear an SCBA and I tell them all the time. You go to a car fire, you go to a bush fire. You go out by the highway, forget about the house fires, wear your mask. You don't want to walk around with what I'm going through. I have no feeling in my face, my shoulder, neck, my arm. I only have eighty percent left in my arm, right arm. And I have no regrets. If I had to do it all over again I would. The guys in New York, I can't imagine what they're going through. You know, losing one guy after another, one guy after another. I don't really ever mention anything to the guys in the field other than the people that know me. They're all new. All the older guys are officers or union officials. They know what I went through and they're behind me all the way. So I have a lot of support between my family and this family, the fire department family.

Gail: I didn't really go to any of the funerals. Can't really tell you why, but I didn't. There was so many of them. I think I went to maybe a couple, one or two. But there were so many of them it was daunting. I know there was a big group of Newark that went to just about every one of them. I give them a lot of credit for that, but I didn't really go to that many, believe it or not. Not that I didn't care or anything like that. It sounds kind of cold and callus that I didn't go, but I really don't know why. Can't really remember why. It was my state of mind I guess.

I've been to the museum. They did a nice job over there. You know it looks very nice. I go to with a big group that goes to the Steven Stiller run. That's the marathon. The tunnel to towers run. That's an impressive event. They got all that together, the story of the guy that they honor. Doing that marathon is great. It's a good fund raiser, but it's a good way to remember him and have a good time at the same time, you know. Good balance.

I don't think I'm really bothered by it more than anybody else. Just sensitive to the fact that it happened. That's about it. I wouldn't say that me being a firefighter made me any more upset, maybe it did. I don't know. At the time it did, but now a days, as I'm getting older.

I don't think it makes me any more upset about it, any more as an American or as a greater New York area resident. That's what aggravates me the most. Because I live here. Because I'm an American, not so much because I'm a firefighter. That's a big part of it too, but I think everybody's upset with what happened to the fire department over there, not just me. But I think being an American makes me more upset about what happened. Just the fact of what they did to us, the whole thing.

Prachar: After that it was just funeral after funeral after memorial service. Then through the pipe band I ended up hooking up with the Port Authority guys. Basically from October through January, when I was off I was on the road going to a funeral or a memorial service somewhere. We were with the Port Authority, they were leaving out of Journal Square, out of the PATH headquarters. I'd drive up with a couple of guys from down here. Drive up to Jersey City, hop on a bus, and off we went. You know, a couple of memorial services a day.

Nasta: I went back once and this was a number of years ago when they had just finished the reflecting pool. The museum wasn't opened yet. That was difficult. I got to say it was difficult to go back there. I went back. I was with my wife and kids. I still can't. I would love to see the museum. I just can't bring myself to go back. So I have not. Eventually I'll take a day, maybe a spur of the moment thing. I'll go over to look at it, but it's a tough place to go back to. I can only speak for myself and I know it's true of a lot of guys.

Rodrigues: I still remember that day like it happened yesterday. It was one of the worst days of my life. Seeing all these people, all American, you know that are getting killed over I guess religious beliefs or political beliefs. It was a really bad, really bad, bad experience.

DeCeuster: I came home after the third day and went to a bar. I sat in a bar, had a drink, and I lost it. I'm crying my ass off at a bar. It took me years to go back. I didn't go back until recently. And I worked there. I used to work downtown. I used to go to the World Trade Center to go to work. Only years later I went. I took a Navy buddy. We went to the Intrepid. So we took that water taxi that went there. It used to be the motorcycle rides over there, but I said, "That's okay." I don't know why. I wasn't afraid of it. Don't get me wrong. I didn't have a need to go. So I finally got to go. I took my buddy over there after years and years of that. It wasn't that it was like a traumatic part. I mean, there were fingers, there was shit all over the place, but what I took away was the work, the cohesiveness of everybody working together. The iron workers, that's a different breed of man. I guess it was everybody working there. But it just was people working together. It amazed me. Really good to see.

Daly: I think New York bothered me the most. 9/11, that bothered me the most. I was a wreck for a couple of days after I went over there and I came back. I was like a zombie.

That affected me a great deal, to this day I think about it. I can't wear a shirt that says remember 9/11. I can't watch any movie that says 9/11. I can't watch the one with the airplane, Flight ninety-two. I can't have anything to do with it. When I see people exploiting that, it really gets me pissed off. I want to just smack them. I take it very much to heart and I donate a lot of money. There's an AC soccer club down by us; they have a Thanksgiving Day tournament. I asked permission to do a fund raiser. I put the pictures of all the firemen that died on placards. I raised close to I think it was nine thousand dollars and the soccer club gave me two thousand more. The state association gave me three thousand more. That went all over to the parents, to the wives and kids. It was like close to fifteen thousand dollars and it made me feel a little bit better, but not totally. 9/11 just really hit home. It just whacked me right out.

Tarantino: I did not attend any funerals or memorials. I knew one or two New York City guys and obviously it made everybody sad, but I didn't want to become afraid of being a fireman, so I did not attend one funeral. I didn't go to one memorial. Somebody asked me this a couple of years ago. Did you regret not going and I said, you know what, I don't regret not going to any of them because I think it might have changed me as a fireman. I think it was better for me not to go. It might just be selfish, looking at it introspectively, but I think I would have made the same decision today. I think only being on the job twelve years. I think it would have changed my whole perspective. I had only been to a couple of Masses, like I went to DeLane's Mass.

Line of duty, nobody likes it, but I really didn't like it. I really didn't like it. I think it kind of stayed in my head a little bit. So I didn't go to any of the memorial stuff, not one thing.

I do that tunnel to tower run. I've probably done it about eight, nine times. First time I did it, I did it with Ernie Lunetta and Ozzy Robetto. There were probably three, four thousand people there. Now it's this whole big event. It's on Channel Two. We have pictures. I mean it's great. That kid Eddie Paulo, he's really taken it under his belt and run with it. Now we literally start that race. The tunnel to tower run that they run it every year, Eddie about three, four years ago, five years ago, ended up hooking up with a representative of Steven Stiller, the kid who did that tunnel thing. We go in full turnout gear, the whole thing. We go and do the run every year. But literally they know us now. So now when they start the race, we're at the front, at the starting line. Newark is at the front. It's actually pretty cool. It's really cool.

I registered for that World Trade Center registry. Just to make sure nothing happened to me. They send me that questionnaire every year. But thank God nothing's happened to me. I'd be lying if I said I thought about it a lot.

Sorace: I guess it was about 2005 when I was first started having symptoms of something wrong along with a handful of other guys that responded with me. Turns out after testing, I had thyroid cancer. I think my first surgery was in 2006. I pretty much left that surgery thinking, "Oh everything is good. They got everything. I'm good. I'm good to go the rest of my life." Then a year after that, turns around I had to have my second surgery. Again, I'm coming out of surgery thinking all right, good, I'm good to go now. I figure hopefully I'll have a normal life and then I guess it was probably ten months later when I finally got hooked up with the doctors at Sloan and Kettering. They ran some more tests. He says, "Oh, no, no, no, you got to come back in here right away, the cancer is running all around in your neck. You got to come in for a pretty serious surgery. So I went into that surgery in 2008. After the surgery, the proactive doctor at Sloan and Kettering says, "From that surgery we're going to follow you up with the radiation." So I had six weeks of radiation treatments for every single day laid there on that table and basically just get burnt from my nose down to just above my nipple line for six weeks. After about the third day of that, you're literally burning inside your mouth, your throat, your tongue, your gums, everything, it was unbearable to swallow anything, even saliva.

So I think within the first couple of weeks I lost like forty-seven pounds from not eating or even being able to eat or drink since day three. I mean extreme, extremely painful, twenty-four seven, no relief at any way. I was literally on four different pain killers. I had a patch that I was wearing. I was taking two liquid pain killers and plus pill pain killers and none of it would put a dent in it. The doctors would explain to me that the head and neck radiation is probably the worst radiation you can ever get. So, it was hell for probably eight months. Because after the radiation, I said, "Oh great it's over, it's over." But they said after the radiation the pain just gets worse and worse and worse. And boy it did. It was just unbearable. I lost so much weight and I was so weak. Besides going for the radiation every day, I was going back to the hospitals and emergency rooms because I was just dehydrated. I had to go there to get IVs because I could not swallow anything. They were trying not to put a feeding tune into me because it can lead to a bunch of complications. So, when the time came where I just can't take this anymore; you got to put the tube in me. They basically didn't want to because they said, "Oh you're starting to come out of the woods now. We don't want to mess with that tube and all that's involved with it." So I just stuck it out and for months and months and months I was in and out of the hospital. The pain, you can't imagine. I couldn't even swallow saliva. Couldn't sleep, couldn't cry because it hurt so bad.

It took probably a year. I lost my taste for probably eight months. I had no taste at all. I'm back to work here in the firehouse since October 2008 after being out six months for the third surgery and the radiation. I came back and I still have like loads and loads and loads of side effects. I have what they call dysphagia, difficulty swallowing. So the third surgery they did what they call a radical left neck dissection where they took out part of the muscles, a vein, and part of a saliva gland on the left side. So I have less saliva. Between the combination of the radiation and the muscles that they took out, what you might swallow in one swallow takes me four swallows with a sip of water or a sip of something. All right so like crazy, crazy side effects that I have, I have them for the rest of my life, the swallowing, the head movement and stuff like that. But I learned when I was in the hospital in New York it really sucks, but I see these little kids walking in the hallway and they're ten times worse than I am. Half of their faces are cut off from cancer. I'm fortunate that I can do what I can do now.

I've been documented. It was from 9/11, so when I got a bill in the mail years ago from Blue Cross Blue Shield that said I had reached my lifetime maximum benefits, I was shocked. I never knew there was such a thing. Fortunately now, because it was due from 9/11 the government is taking care of a good part of the medical bills, the medical monitoring, and following. Still on medication the rest of my life. The discomfort and stuff that people probably don't see I'm going through twenty-four/seven. When I sleep because I have less saliva, it's like you're trying to sleep with dry mouth. So you're waking up every five minutes. But anyway I'm fortunate that I'm still doing what I'm doing. So, I'm thankful for all my friends and the job that's still here. There's always somebody worse than me, right?

The thing is when this was going on over there the EPA said, "Oh yeah the qualities are good. Everything's good. Everything's good." And by all means, us as members of the task force, we have our own haz-mat guys that are checking the air, checking the air. So it wasn't like we skimp on anything. We wore our proper dust mask and stuff that we were instructed to wear. It just happened. It killed how many thousand people that day. Now people are dying every day from it still.

Bartelloni: We did go to a few memorials. We had the one here in Newark. New York Fire Commissioner Von Essen came out. I think he was a union guy that became Commissioner. He came here in Newark, so we had something here. I know Chief Centanni was friendly with him and we did something downtown. He actually came because I think he realized how many people from Newark were out there. A lot of guys went out there, so he came and they did a memorial. I can't remember where it was. Somewhere downtown, but it was good. It was a little bit after that. I don't remember if it was six months later. It wasn't that close. Maybe it was within the year. But he came out and we had a good day. We had a lot of guys show up. We had the trucks and he spoke. It was good that they appreciated all the work that everybody put in.

I have no health issues. The only thing that I can really think of and I've always had sinus issues, but that day my head was just pounding from that smoke. And it was just that I'm sensitive to smoke. Here being a fireman, I'm sensitive to smoke. Hard to believe, but I've been to a lot of fires here where my head doesn't pound. When I came back to the firehouse that night, I couldn't even get out of bed. We stayed here no matter what. We worked, but my head was absolutely pounding. Whatever was in that smoke that day and obviously we're seeing people dying today and the fund and all of that, it wasn't good. That day I knew because I'm sensitive to it, something was up and I knew. Christy Whitman declared that it was safe. Obviously, there're a lot of dead people. Not that they wouldn't be there. I think no matter what, there were kids in there and your fellow firefighters; they're going to go anyway. But maybe there was a precaution they could have taken. When you clear it for people, it's good enough for them. They wanted to be there so people are still dying from it. Kids I think that were in a school that they brought back too soon. From what I heard some of them are in other states, dying, sick. So there's no coincidence. We got a few guys here that are coming down with different things. They worked with the urban search and rescue; they had cancer, thyroid. There's no question where it came from.

I've been to the museum. Amazing, having those firetrucks down there and the beams that they have. I took my wife and we took pictures. Then we went to O'Hare's Pub, with all firemen patches throughout. It was pretty much on the corner. Right down the street from it and people have been coming from all over and leaving their patches. So I did. It was impressive. I had an impressive day, with the tapes and they had a whole bunch of different things, sights, sounds. So it was good. It was impressive. It was the whole complex. They did a tremendous job like New York would do.

Brownlee: Went to a hundred funerals. Went to ones out in Westchester, ones out in Staten Island, ones out in Long Island, went all over. A lot of the times I went Jeffery Dixon to the funerals. I didn't go on the bus or on the rig or anything like that, we just went over in uniform.

I still have not been over to the museum. Don't want to do it, eventually maybe, but right now, no. I did go to a thing in Liberty

State Park. We went over there with the fire department honor guard. Jersey City was all pissed off because our honor guard was on the stage with Lou Rawls and the Rawlettes and they had to stay outside and it was in Jersey City. They were all pissed off about that. But hey, shit happens.

Partridge: It was an extremely emotional time for me. You know as the days went on I was getting a clear picture of the friends that I had lost. In addition to the firefighters, a guy that I went to high school with and had known for years and years and years and who was a volunteer firefighter with me. He had also been working in one of the insurance companies in the Trade Center and had been killed that day. So there was a lot going on. It was almost too much to absorb. I think being on the job you kind of get trained to compartmentalize in order to be able to do your job. I think that's what we were doing. You don't let yourself feel a lot of things. You just focus on the moment, whatever you're doing.

I was always very good at that. I can let myself think about it if I want to. I can experience it in whatever way I want to or not. I was always good at that on the job. Putting something aside and being able to move past it. I don't know what long term effects there are, but I don't have any kind of PTSD or anything like that. I know that for a fact, from that or from our job. So sometime if I want to think about Terry or Joey or the guys from Rescue Three where I hung out a lot or the guys from Rescue One where I hung out a lot, I can do that. I can do that. Sometimes I think about what we actually did there at the site.

I can do that too. And then other times I just say, "Okay, It was a long thirty years and that was part of it."

But I went to a lot of funerals. I went to some funerals for friends of mine. I couldn't get to all the funerals. Like I said, I lost seventeen. I couldn't get to all those funerals because in some cases I was working. In some cases there were too many funerals to go to at one time and I had to pick and choose. And in some cases I went to funerals for guys that I never knew because we were trying to make sure that every funeral had a strong fire department presence. Went to funerals in Staten Island. Went to funerals in upstate New York. So I don't remember how many I went to.

The worst one probably was Terry Hatten. He had been the captain at Rescue One. He was a good friend of mine. I had known him since he was a new fireman in Rescue Two in Brooklyn. We had been friends for a long, long time. I had seen him not long before 9/11 and his funeral was held in Saint Patrick's. It was a pretty big deal. Giuliani had married Terry and his wife. His wife was one of Giuliani's main assistants. There were a lot of moving parts to that funeral. It was a big deal and it was a very emotional one. I think that was the worst one for me because of all the guys I knew that day, I had known him and this other guy, Joey Angelini. He was actually the senior firefighter in the entire FDNY. He was in Rescue One and he was like sixty-four and change, a couple of months away from being dragged out the door kicking and screaming. He died that day as did his son, but Joey and Terry were probably the two worst for me because I knew them the best.

I didn't do the tunnel to tower run. I had my hands full. The whole 9/11 thing led to me becoming chief and Chief of Special Operations. I had my hands full right up until I retired from the job. Then a year after I retired from the job, I dropped dead of a heart attack. So that pretty much finished me for any kind of tunnel runs or any of that kind of stuff. Plus the reason I got off the job was because my back had fallen apart. I woke up morning basically paralyzed. So between my back and my heart there was nothing physical I was ever going to do. There were a lot of events and affairs over the years that I did go to and every once in a while I still do. But I emotionally spend too much time on this and need to be distanced from it.

For us in Newark it wasn't nearly the hit it was for the guys in the FDNY, obviously. So for guys in Newark to feel the way they did, I can only imagine what the FDNY guys feel like. To this day I have a lot of very, very close friends over there and we talk about it. I just can't imagine. In Newark we lost guys while I was on the job. Mike DeLane was directly in my company, worked with me personally and I remember all the grief over that and multiply that by three forty three. I mean it's just no concept. I have not been to the memorial. I kind of don't want to go. If that makes any sense.

McGovern: I went to quite a few funerals. I don't remember how many, but we tried to get to ones that were nearby, Staten Island or something like that. I think there was one in Jersey we went to. A lot of the guys did that.

I got lymphatic Leukemia, but it's under control right now. I go to the Rutgers WTC clinic once a year for checkups . They concluded it was from the WTC. It's just a matter of waiting, watching, keeping an eye on my blood work. Other than that, I see a cardiologist, oncologists, pulmonologist. You know the drill. But I feel relatively okay.

Homeland security, that came into play. Agencies cooperating with each other which they never did before. And money started coming in for fire departments which was good for equipment.

Montalvo: I know when I came back from there after my second day, I kind of pretty much went to my room and laid down for a good two days. I just went to bed. Just from what I saw going on over there, just the smell too, kind of stuck with me. I spent a good two days in bed. I didn't want to deal with anything after that.

Weidele: I still to this day can't believe we couldn't stop that. You know the devastation, the buildings, and I see all the people that passed away. But it hits home more because we're firemen. We see the three forty three, all the rigs, everything that was damaged.

I think about it to this day, that that could happen again. We're not even at a building collapse, that we can get hurt. You know we think we're invincible and you know there is that chance that you can get hurt. You know people don't tell you on this job. There is a chance you might not come home.

Castelluccio: It made me very angry. It made me an angry person to see something like that happen to our people. And to know that three hundred and forty three brother firefighters gave their lives. Literally, sacrificed themselves to try to help people. I think only firemen could truly understand that or firemen's families, the selflessness of these people. They probably knew that they were going to die going into those buildings. It's something that we do. So, it's something that still lingers with me today. I get mad at how politicians forget, how people forget what went on. And forgive and forget, no, you never forget.

Lee: To be honest with you, to this day I don't watch any of that 9/11 stuff. I don't watch The Towers. I don't watch any because it still brings back a bad feeling.

Burkhardt: But the Trade Center was scary. Seen a lot of shows on it. It's still gets me watching it. I saw how the cops mobilized and we didn't do shit. Then if you went over there they're going to put you on charges. Then you had to deny ever going over there. They finally sent a rig over there to go to the wakes and the funerals. It's just knowing that you just got a box and nobody in it on top of the fire engine. Then they start going through the DNA and find the people and the family's got to go over it again. I don't know. I talked about that to my wife. I said, like if something happens to me on the job, no way I want a fire department thing. I told my wife, when somebody comes knocks on the door and says, do you want, just kick them out and if my father's alive and my brother's alive, you talk to them.

Alexander, Captain Donald, 2 September, 2016, transcript.

Arce, Battalion Chief Orlando, 9 October, 2016, transcript.

Bartelloni, Battalion Chief Paul, August 1, 2019, transcript.

Bellina, Deputy Director of the Office of Emergency Management Frank, 17 August, 2017, transcript.

Brownlee, Battalion Chief Walter, 4 September, 2019, transcript.

Burkhardt, Captain Kevin, 9 February, 2004, transcript.

Castelluccio, Deputy Chief Anthony, 23 August, 2016, transcript

Centanni, Fire Chief John, 9 November, 2016, transcript.

Dainty, Battalion Chief Cliff, 21 June, 2019, transcript

Daly, Captain Philip, 4 September, 2008, transcript.

DeCeuster, Battalion Chief Steven, 22 May, 2019, transcript.

Farrell, Captain Daniel, 30 July, 3 August, 2016, transcript.

Freese, Firefighter Miguel, 11 August, 2016, transcript.

Gail, Deputy Chief Richard, 16 July, 2019, transcript.

Greene, Captain David, July 29, 2019, transcript.

Griffith, Captain Edward, 9 September, 15 October, 2016, transcript.

Griggs, Captain John, 28 September, 2016, transcript.

Highsmith, Firefighter Gregory, 8 August, 2016, transcript.

Jackson, Fire Chief Rufus, 6 August, 2016, transcript.

Johnson, Captain Otis, 21 July, August 14, 2016, transcript.

Killeen, Battalion Chief Kevin, 28 September, 2009, 12 March, 2019, transcript.

Langenbach, Deputy Chief James, 5 July, 2019, transcript.

LaPenta, Captain Steven, 30 September, 2016, transcript.

Lee, Battalion Chief Sylvester, 5 October, 2016, transcript.

Masters, Captain Al, 20 August, 2016, transcript.

McGovern, Battalion Chief Thomas, 19 July, 2019, transcript.

Meier, Captain Donald, 9 August, 2016, transcript.

Montalvo, Firefighter Raymond, 5 August, 2016, transcript.

Nasta, Deputy Chief Michael, 17 June, 2019, transcript.

Ostertag, Captain, Steve, 29 July, 2016, transcript.

Partridge, Battalion Chief Peter, 26 July, 2019, transcript.

Perdon, Captain George, 9 June, 2003, transcript.

Petrone, Firefighter Michael, 23 July, 2016, transcript.

Pierre, Captain Yves, 15 July, 2016, transcript.

Pierson, Captain James, 28 August, 2016, transcript.

Prachar, Captain John, 10 July, 20 September, 2005, transcript.

Ramos, Firefighter Juan, 12 August, 2016, transcript.

Richardson, Captain Scott, 2 August, 2016, transcript.

Roberson, Firefighter Luther, 22 August, 2016, transcript.

Rodrigues, Battalion Chief Deblin, 21 August, 2016, transcript.

Sorace, Captain Michael, 18 August, 2016, transcript.

Sperli, Battalion Chief Joseph, 21 August, 2016, transcript.

Straile, Battalion Chief Joseph, 31 July, 2018, transcript.

Tarantino, Captain Anthony, 27 June, 2019, transcript.

Weidele, Battalion Chief William, 20 July, 2016, transcript.

West, Firefighter Charles, 12 July, 2019, transcript.

Willis, Firefighter James, 9 July, 2019, transcript.

Zieser, Deputy Chief Richard, 25 July, 2016, transcript.

www.ingramcontent.com/pod-product-compliance
Lightning Source LLC
Chambersburg PA
CBHW030011110426
42741CB00032B/328